AF606846

CONNECT DISCONNECT

GROWTH IN THE "IT" CITY

CONNECT / DISCONNECT

GROWTH IN THE "IT" CITY

EDITED BY SHAUN GILES
FOREWORD BY SUSAN H. EDWARDS

Frist Art Museum in association with
Vanderbilt University Press
Nashville, Tennessee

Connect/Disconnect: Growth in the "It" City

Frist Art Museum

Published by the Frist Art Museum
and Vanderbilt University Press

Library of Congress Control
Number: 2019946702
ISBN 978-0-8265-2280-1

Frist Art Museum
Brandon Gnetz, graphic designer
Wallace Joiner, managing editor
Danielle Myers, graphic designer

Vanderbilt University Press
Joell Smith-Borne, managing production editor
Zachary Gresham, editor

Cover illustrations: **FRONT LEFT**: Rae'chel Curtis. *East Nashville Easter Community Outreach* (detail), 2018 **FRONT RIGHT**: Ray Di Pietro. *This Doorway Was His Home* (detail), 2018 **BACK**: John Roeder. *Nashville Skyline East View*, 2013

Published in conjunction with the exhibition *Connect/Disconnect: Growth in the "It" City* (March 22–August 4, 2019) at the Frist Art Museum, Nashville, Tennessee

Jurors
Marty Stuart, musician and photographer
Carlton Wilkinson, educator and photographer
Susan H. Edwards, executive director and CEO, Frist Art Museum

Curators
Shaun Giles
Rosemary Brunton

Exhibition design
Hans Schmitt-Matzen

Graphic design
Brandon Gnetz

Supported in part by our **O'Keeffe Circle members** and

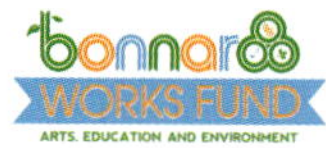

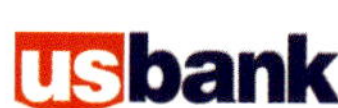

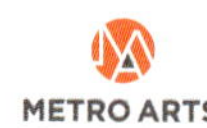

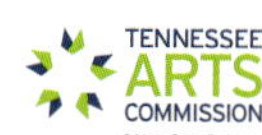

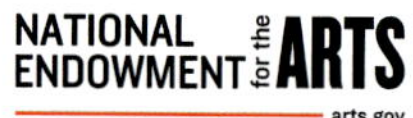

CONTENTS

FOREWORD

In January 2013, the *New York Times* anointed Nashville the nation's "it" city. It was teeming with immigrants, tourists, and transplants lured by jobs, quality of life, entertainment, and the growing food, fashion, and film scenes. Nashville had been at the top of various lists for several years, including being the number one destination for business relocation and one of the best places to begin a technology start-up. The late journalist John Egerton, who had lived in Nashville since the 1970s, said at the time, "We ought to be paying more attention to how many people we have who are ill-fed and ill-housed and ill-educated."

By 2018, it was estimated that 100 people were moving to the Nashville metropolitan statistical area every day. Assistant director for community engagement Shaun Giles and educator for community engagement Rosemary Brunton noticed that neighborhoods were changing and that the rapid growth was straining the city's infrastructure. Although many were prospering, and the creative culture was making an impact locally, they wondered: What was drawing new people to Nashville? How did lifelong residents feel about the city's transformation and their place in it? Was Nashville still a welcoming place?

Wanting to provide a platform for people to share their views, Giles and Brunton issued a call to photographers living in Davidson County—professional or amateur, fine art or commercial—to submit photos that address connection or disconnection in the new Nashville. Nearly two hundred digital images were submitted by more than one hundred qualified residents. Entertainer and photographer Marty Stuart, professor and photographer Carlton Wilkinson, and I served as jurors. We selected fifty photographs to be exhibited in the Conte Community Arts Gallery at the Frist Art Museum in the spring and early summer of 2019.

The exhibition, *Connect/Disconnect: Growth in the "It" City*, offers a balanced record of a moment in history and gives voice to a democratic cross section of the city's residents. Soaring steel and glass structures sprout up on previously vacant lots or adjacent to the horizontal architecture of the past, altering the skyline, vistas, and streetscapes. Cranes dot the horizon, and construction workers find full employment.

Hope for the future is seen in the optimism of children at play. A diverse group of children burst from the starting gate to hunt for eggs on an Easter morning in East Nashville. A woman wearing a burqa provides a free flu shot to a man with Asian features. Yes, we can all get along, and perhaps even defuse a hostile and polarized political climate with genuine concern for the welfare of others.

Images of Music Row, the Station Inn, and Lower Broadway honor tradition and remind viewers of the countless musicians, vocalists, and songwriters who arrive with a dream. Their tireless commitment to success gives Nashville character and supplies it with entertainment options from listening rooms to concert stages. Music is central to life in Nashville, luring tourists and transplants to its halls and clubs while providing a livelihood for technicians and scholars as well as performers.

Several of the photographs in *Connect/Disconnect* address the topics John Egerton called to our attention in 2013. By 2018, the homeless population in Nashville had risen to nearly three thousand. Two public transit plans had been defeated, and congestion had increased to an uncomfortable and inconvenient degree, gnarling traffic and slowing daily commutes.

Environmental degradation and the loss of green space are poignantly considered in a photograph displaying mounds of accumulated waste occupying the foreground while skyscrapers sprawl across the distant horizon line. "Mounds" also refers to the dwellings of early Middle Tennessee inhabitants. We acknowledge that we occupy the traditional land of the Cherokee, Chickasaw, Choctaw, Creek, Mississippi, and Shawnee people, and we pay respect to their elders past and present. Yet, in the twenty-first century, "mounds" no longer refers to shelter, but rather to urban waste and possibly non-biodegradable landfill, which further scar the natural world that Native people once occupied.

The photographs in *Connect/Disconnect* are conversation starters—nostalgia for some, eye-opening revelations for others. This publication provides literal snapshots of Nashville as seen by fifty residents of Davidson County.

Photography stops time. It records in irrecoverable past. The images published herein reveal a chapter in the story of a city in transition. Some images are a call to action. Others delight and inspire a knowing smile. The photographs will be added to an archive maintained for posterity by the Nashville Public Library's Special Collections Division.

Future generations will one day look at the photographs of *Connect/Disconnect* through a new and knowing lens. How did Nashville and Davidson County respond to the issues of affordable housing, public education, rapid transit, and environmental protection? Did Nashville remain a welcoming community with safe, walkable neighborhoods? Were businesses able to find a highly skilled, well-trained workforce? How long did Nashville retain the title of the nation's "it" city? *Connect/Disconnect* provides a baseline for answering these questions. For now, our neighbors have turned their cameras on us and asked us to join the conversation and picture the future we want for ourselves.

Susan H. Edwards, PhD
Executive Director & CEO

ACKNOWLEDGMENTS

The publication in 2018 of *We Shall Overcome: Press Photographs of Nashville during the Civil Rights Era* confirmed that books related to exhibitions in the Conte Community Arts Gallery at the Frist Art Museum were of wide interest and historical significance. In response, we are producing books to accompany more exhibitions, beginning with *Connect/Disconnect: Growth in the "It" City* and *Murals of North Nashville Now*. For these publications, we are grateful and honored to have the support of Vanderbilt University Press.

The Conte Community Arts Gallery at the Frist Art Museum is reserved for exhibitions of significance to the area, mostly involving artists who reside in Nashville. *Connect/Disconnect: Growth in the "It" City* qualifies because of the premise as well as the participants. Assistant director for community engagement Shaun Giles and educator for community engagement Rosemary Brunton called for submissions from photographers living in Davidson County of images that expressed their feelings of connection or disconnection as a result of the rapid growth in Nashville.

Giles and Brunton received nearly two hundred entries from more than one hundred photographers. Three jurors selected fifty photographs for the exhibition. We thank entertainer and photographer Marty Stuart and educator and photographer Carlton Wilkinson for working with me, the third juror. We appreciate their time and expertise. Following the close of the exhibition, the photographs will be archived at the Nashville Public Library in the Special Collections Division. Special gratitude is due to our colleagues and friends at the library: Kent Oliver, director; Andrea Blackman, manager of the Special Collections Division; and Tasneem Tewogbola, associate director of programming in the Special Collections Division.

At Vanderbilt University Press, we are very grateful to Gianna Mosser, director; Zack Gresham, acquisitions editor, and the copy editor of this book; Joell Smith-Borne, managing production editor; and Betsy Phillips, marketing and sales manager. Their professionalism makes everything easier. The imprimatur of Vanderbilt University Press is not taken for granted. We are grateful for their commitment to the community as well as scholarship. At the Frist Art Museum, we thank Wallace Joiner, managing editor, who as our liaison with Vanderbilt keeps everyone on time and on task. Special thanks to Frist editor Peg Duthie for her attention to detail and commitment to excellence at all times.

For their generous support of the exhibition *Connect/Disconnect*, we thank the Frist Art Museum's O'Keeffe Circle members, the Bonnaroo Works Fund, and the U.S. Bank Foundation. For general operating support, we gratefully acknowledge the generosity of the Frist Foundation, the Metro Arts Commission, the Tennessee Arts Commission, and the National Endowment for the Arts. We also want to express our appreciation to the Frist Art Museum trustees—especially Billy Frist, president and chair—for their encouragement and faith in our abilities to fulfill the mission and vision of the Frist Art Museum.

Neither the exhibition nor this publication would have been possible without the inspirational leadership and compassion of Frist Art Museum educators. We gratefully acknowledge director of education engagement Anne Henderson, Shaun Giles, and Rosemary Brunton. Giles and Brunton served as organizing curators for the exhibition, and Giles is the editor of this publication. We thank them for wearing many hats and for their tireless advocacy for people of all abilities and backgrounds in the Metro Nashville area. Our greatest debt, of course, is to the photographers who took the time to submit work and share their stories.

Susan H. Edwards, PhD
Executive Director & CEO

CONNECT/DISCONNECT

Nashville's rapid development is the current chapter in the history of a city which has seen its share of change. Historical markers are reminders of Nashville's role in the Civil War as well as the civil rights movement. The adoption of metropolitan government in 1962 redefined the city. Natural events such as the devastating tornado of 1998 and the unprecedented flood in 2010 reshaped lives and neighborhoods. These moments are parts of Nashville's story, and photography is one way this history has been preserved. With cameras more accessible than they have ever been, all citizens, whether professional photographers, amateurs, or hobbyists, have the ability to capture unique images of their surroundings. With this in mind, the Frist Art Museum organized a photography call and culminating exhibition intended to provide a forum for sharing photographs and perspectives of the city's growth.

Over one hundred Nashvillians submitted to an open call for photographs documenting the city's transition and the ways in which the change is enabling connection or disconnection among local communities. The fifty photographers selected for the exhibition *Connect/Disconnect: Growth in the "It" City* come with different lived experiences, points of view, and levels of proficiency.

David S. Piñeros arrived in Nashville in 2017 to work for the Tennessee Department of Environment and Conservation. He is an emerging documentary photographer whose work primarily focuses on ecological, cultural, and social issues. He has exhibited in multiple art venues and galleries in Nashville and has published a book of his photography.

In contrast to Piñeros, Bernadette Hugan, a Nashville resident since the mid-1980s, describes herself as a "passionate photography novice" who attended a community education digital photography foundations class in 2017 and has continued learning about the process.

Like Hugan, Yukiko Ueda is new to photography. Her family immigrated to Nashville from Japan in 1987 to further her partner's graduate study. She took up photography only in 2018 but does have a background in art and is enrolled in the MFA program at the School of the Art Institute of Chicago.

Emily Passino grew up working in the darkroom with her dad. She moved to Nashville from Knoxville in 1978 as a young wife and mother and still lives in the house they bought in 1981. She started more deliberate study about ten years ago and has had a number of photos selected for various juried local shows, but still says, "I'm constantly learning, and only recently comfortable with the idea of identifying as a photographer."

Each photograph in the exhibition is a unique observation of Nashville. Some images capture the connection of shared community and the opportunities that come with urban progress; others highlight the disconnect experienced by those left behind by rapid growth.

Several photographers chose to highlight connection in the "it" city through photographs that encapsulate the optimism of a community that is growing at a rate of one hundred people per day, lifelong residents who see change and are excited by what's to come, people who have found community among their neighbors, and those who are embracing change by meeting challenges with solutions. Alan Hayes's *Street Mural in East Nashville* highlights the Tomato Art Fest, an annual event that has become part of the fabric of East Nashville over the past fifteen years, by capturing artist Troy Duff as he puts finishing touches on a tomato-themed street mural.

Tony Gonzalez took his photograph *Visioning* while on assignment with Nashville Public Radio in 2016. "The event was specifically intended to gather community thoughts about transportation and urban planning along Nolensville Pike—and to do so in a targeted way with the Somali community." Gonzalez explains embracing the challenge of change. "My image does show how people are dealing with growing pains, but they are doing so in a proactive way to try to guide the future of their community. It also bucks a little bit against the kind of cynicism that many people and many Nashvillians have about the future, believing there's nothing to be done about change, or that it has to be an anonymous, oppressive, inevitable change."

The photographers also considered those who are disconnected and disheartened by the rapid growth and the consequences of overpopulation, people who can no longer afford to live in neighborhoods that they have always called home, and the most vulnerable among us who are experiencing homelessness.

Ray Di Pietro, a sixteen-year resident of Nashville, captured *This Doorway Was His Home* after observing a man living in the Sheraton Hotel's service doorway for an extended period. "He lived in that doorway for weeks, through CMA Music Festival, unnoticed by hordes of residents, office workers, and tourists walking by. To me, it was a jarring moment of change in Nashville and that's what I was looking to capture and convey."

In *Under the Music City,* David Piñeros documents "three major issues that are linked with each other: overpopulation, consumerism, and garbage. The picture is about fast human growth and the blindness from this society, which is a form of disconnection."

Many of the photographers' observations are not easily categorized, but rather invite viewers to form their own conclusions.

Grandfathered Inn is Betty Harper's photograph of a beloved Nashville institution, Station Inn, located in the Gulch, an area that has undergone remarkable transformation in recent years. Harper, who moved to Nashville in 1969 with her husband and two children, has watched Nashville change over the years. "We enjoy going to the Station Inn on Tuesday nights for the Doyle & Debbie Show and this particular evening I had my camera in the car. As we opened the door I looked up and noticed the sign and immediately was aware of the new world popping up around the Inn. With all the new construction in the Gulch, the Station Inn is somewhat of a welcome relic."

In 2019, Nashville continues to emerge as a major American city. It has become a desirable destination for individuals, families, and businesses. Still considered the "Music City," Nashville is growing beyond that designation and becoming a cultural center. Unfortunately, this has placed great strain on its infrastructure and, as the city's profile has risen, so has the cost of living. Several neighborhoods have become desirable destinations for residents and small businesses, often at the expense of those who have lived there the longest. Nashville can celebrate its growth, but it is important to be prepared for the challenges that come with it. Once this city on the rise becomes a fully realized vision, the photographs from *Connect/Disconnect* will serve as reminders of how the city managed and adapted to change.

Shaun Giles

PLATES

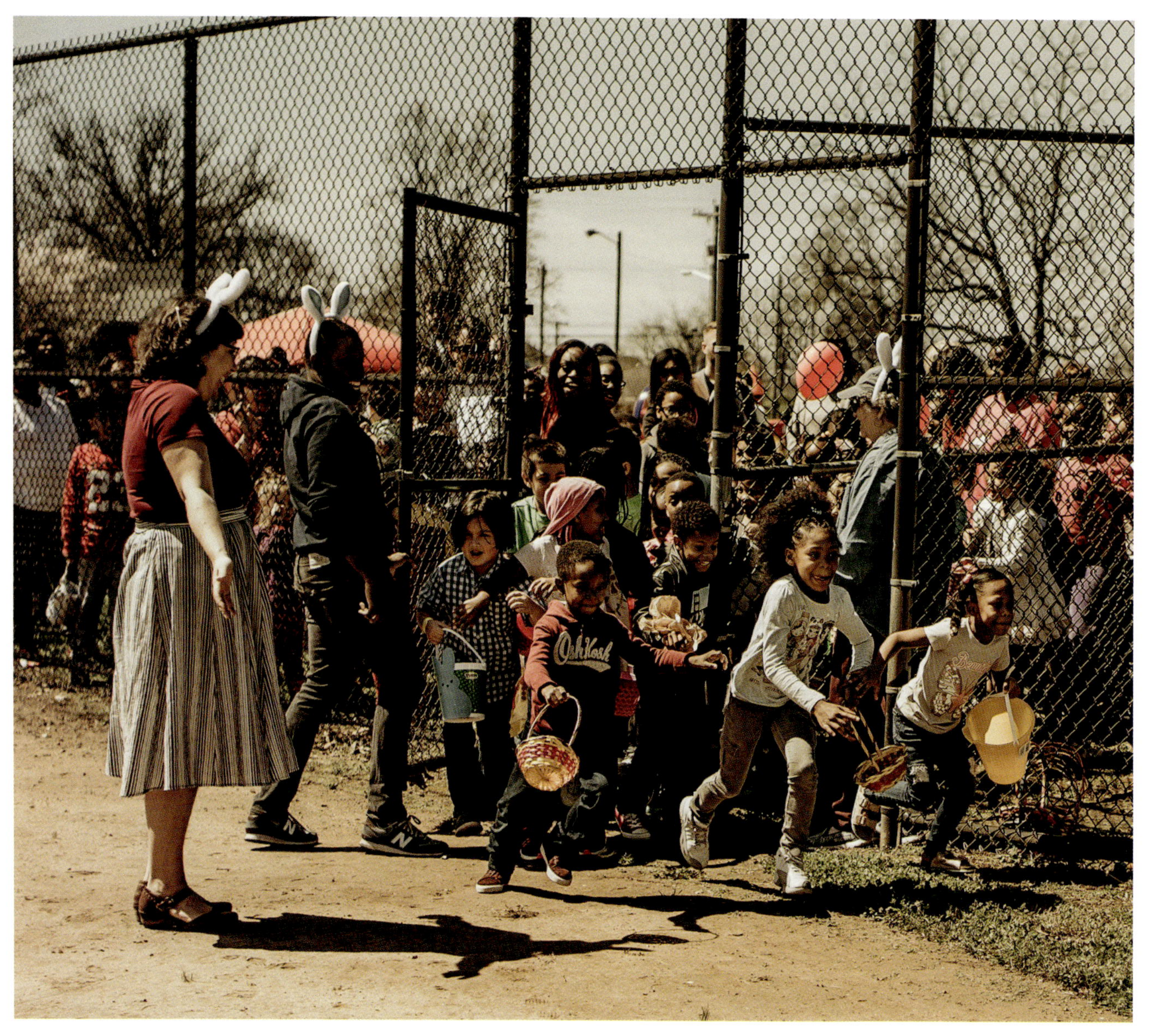

Rae'chel Curtis
East Nashville Easter Community Outreach, 2018

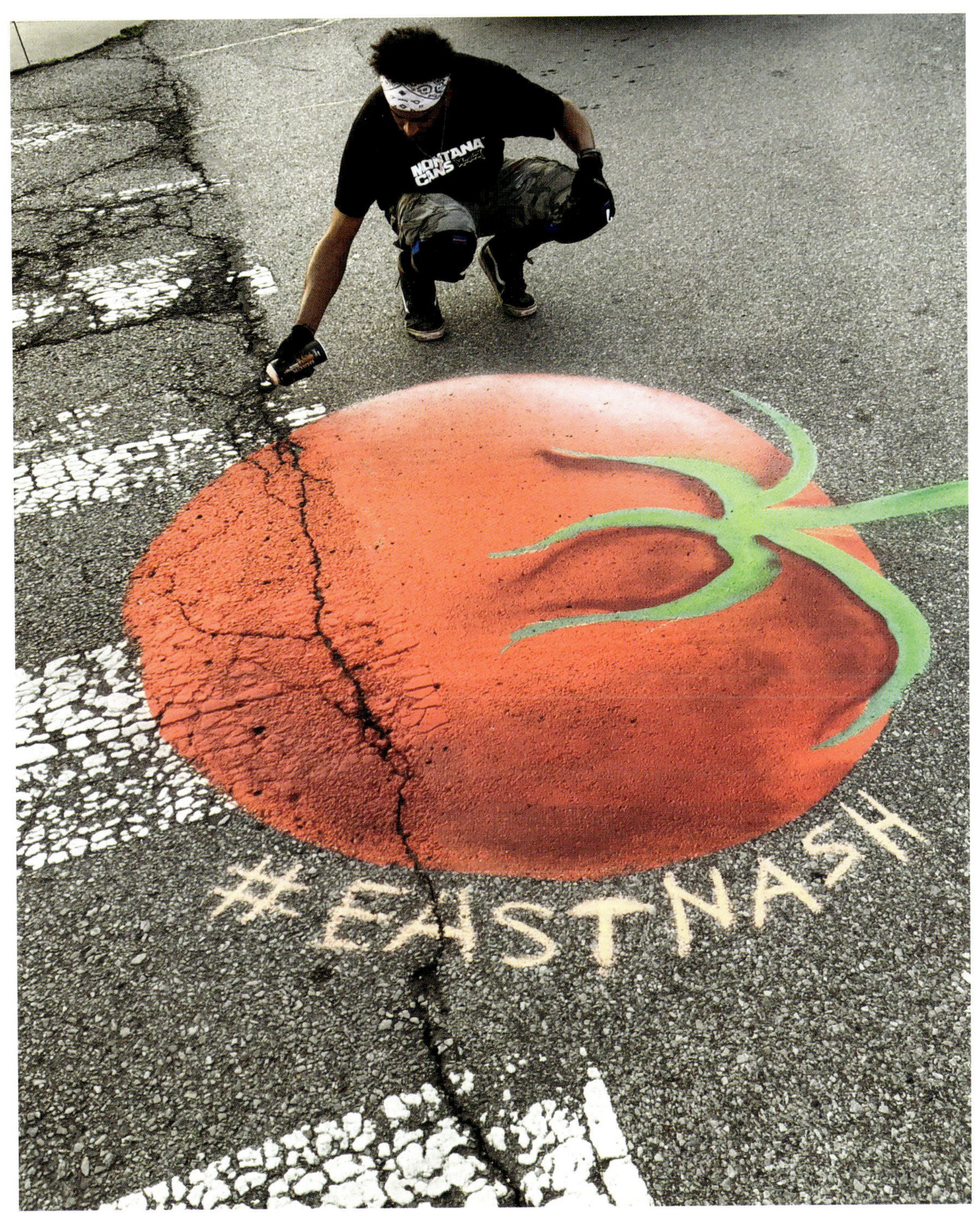

Alan Hayes
Street Mural in East Nashville, 2018

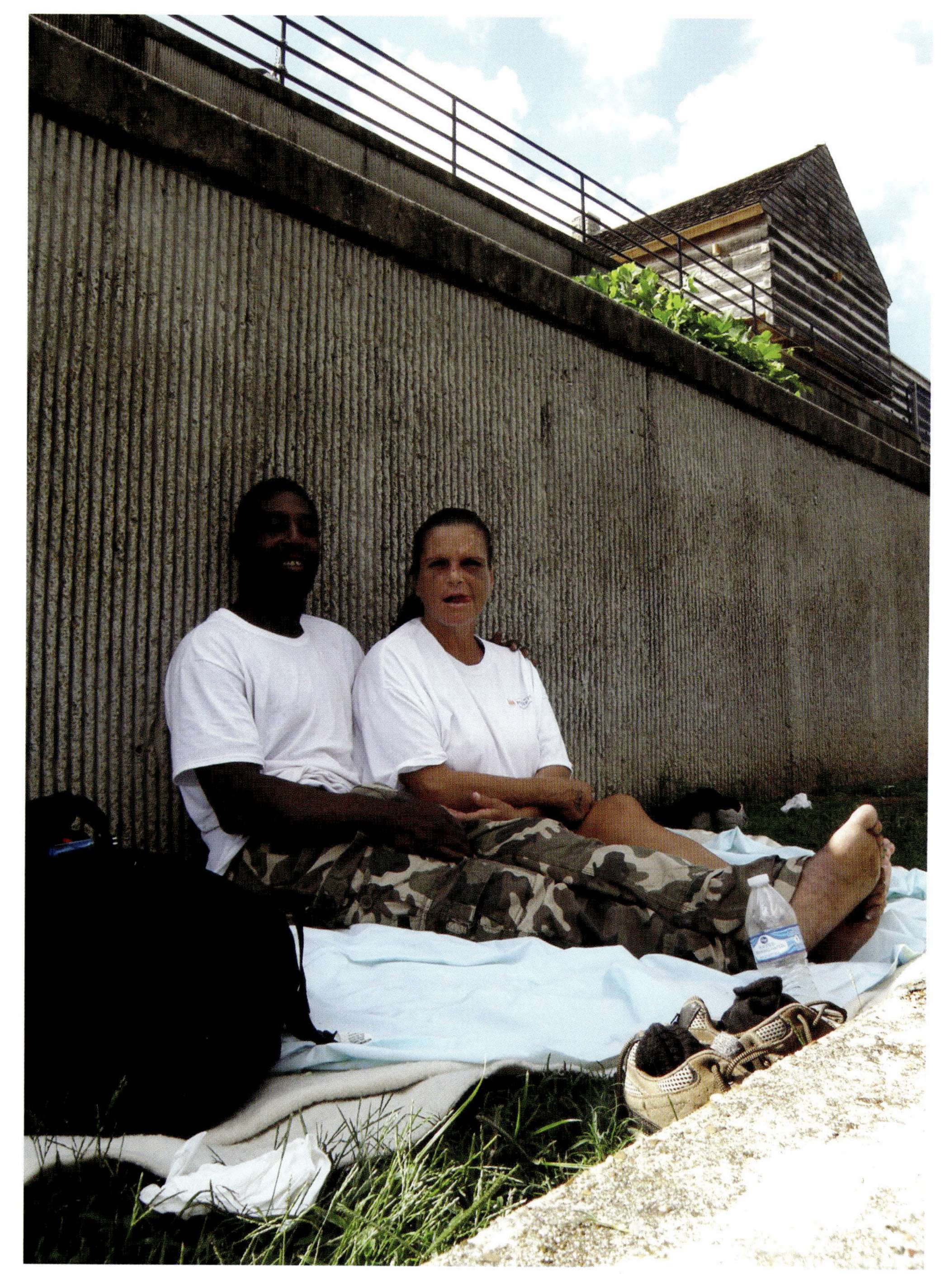

Holly Abernathy
Listening to the Game Across the River, 2018

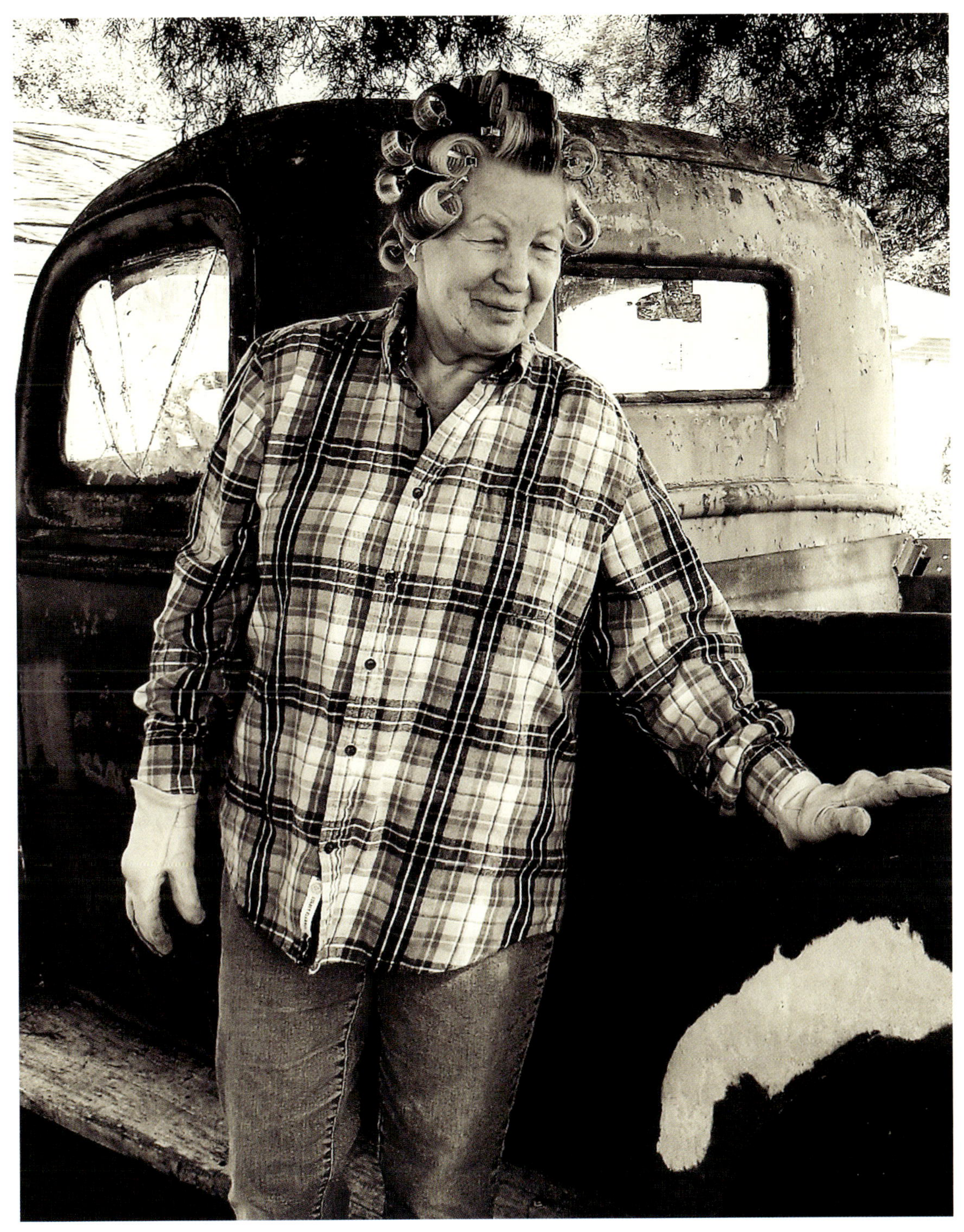

Erin McDermott
Working Woman, 2018

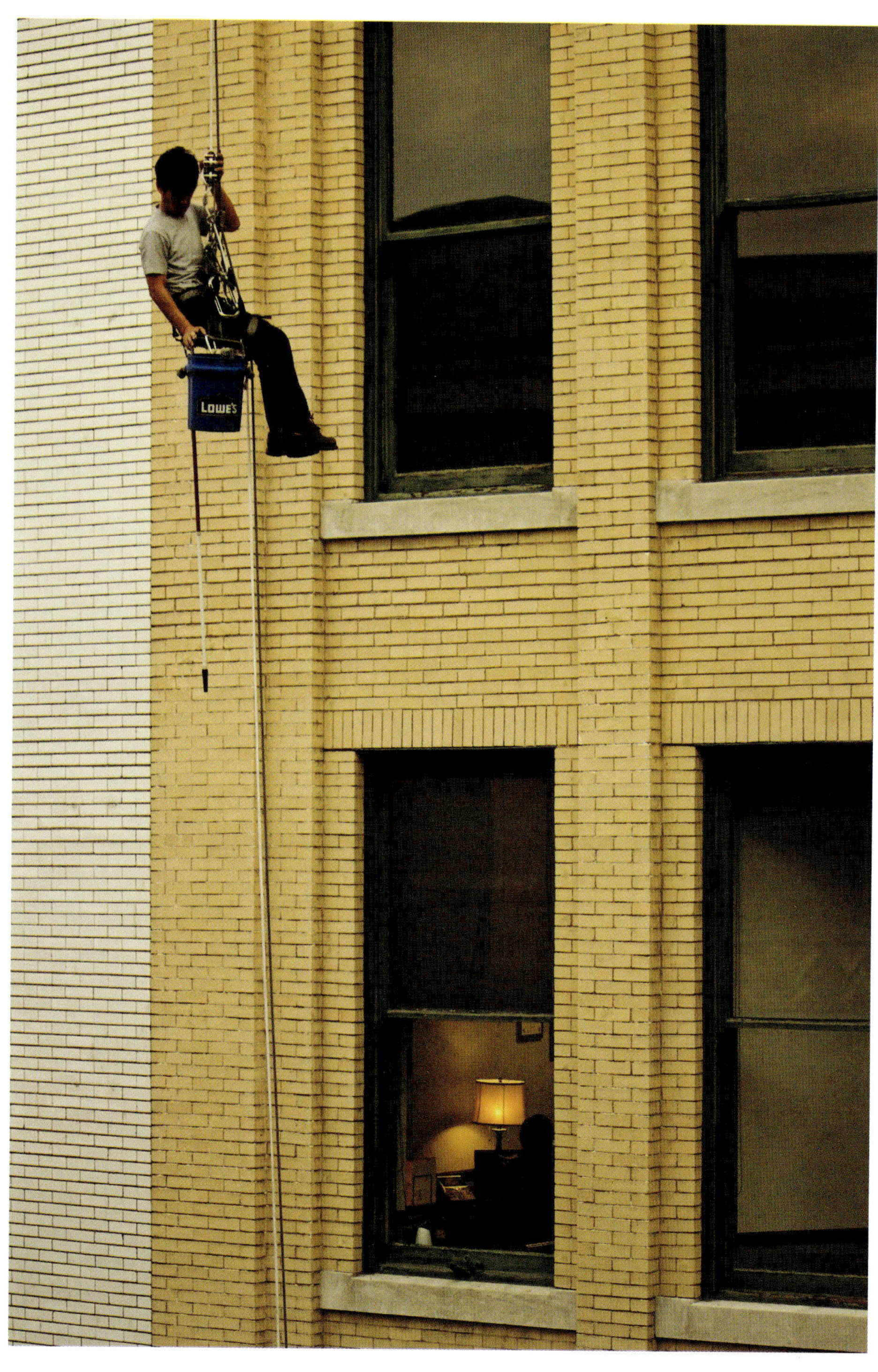

Bernadette Hugan
Tethered, 2018

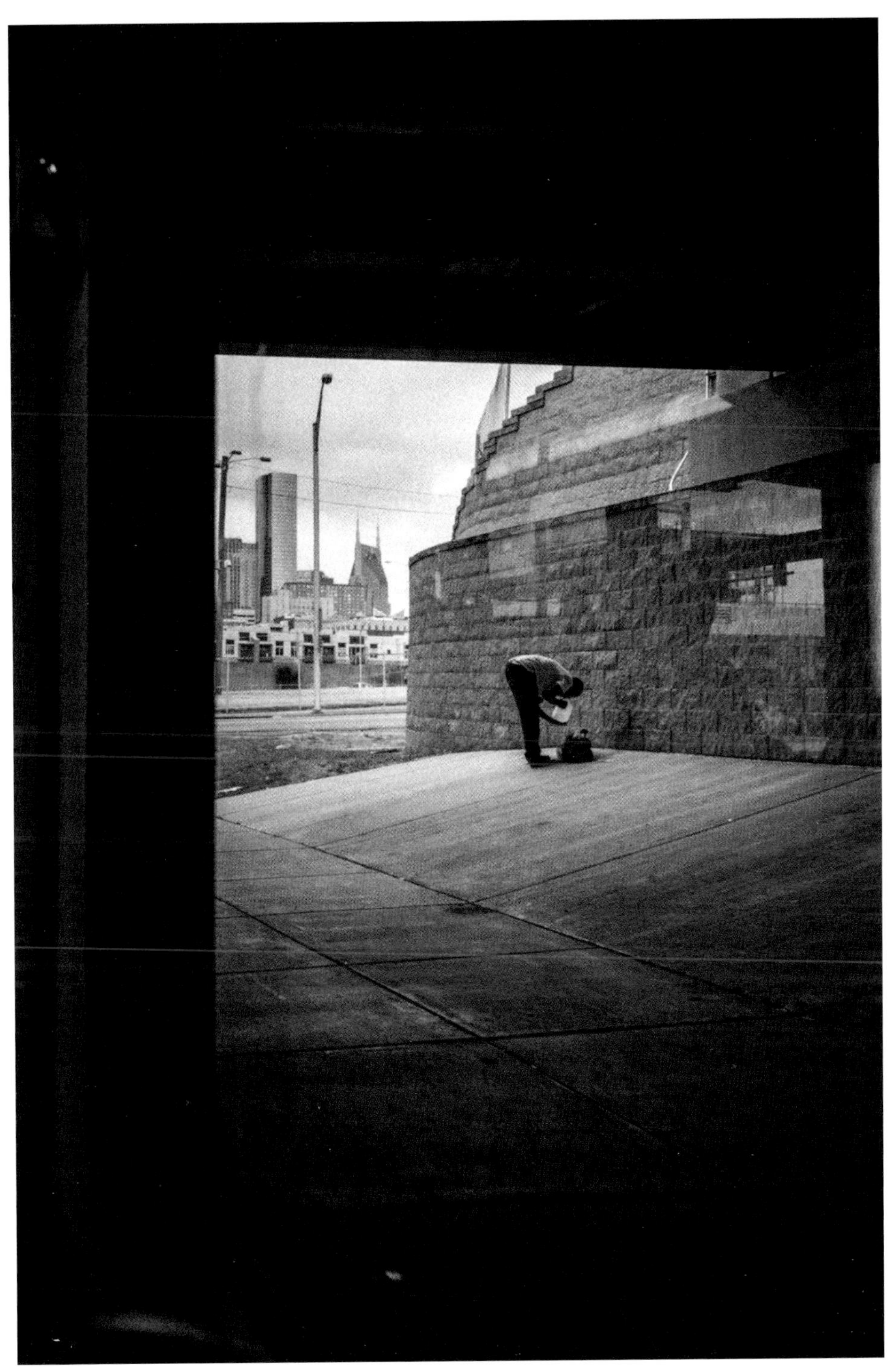

Joshua Ness
The Outskirts, 2018

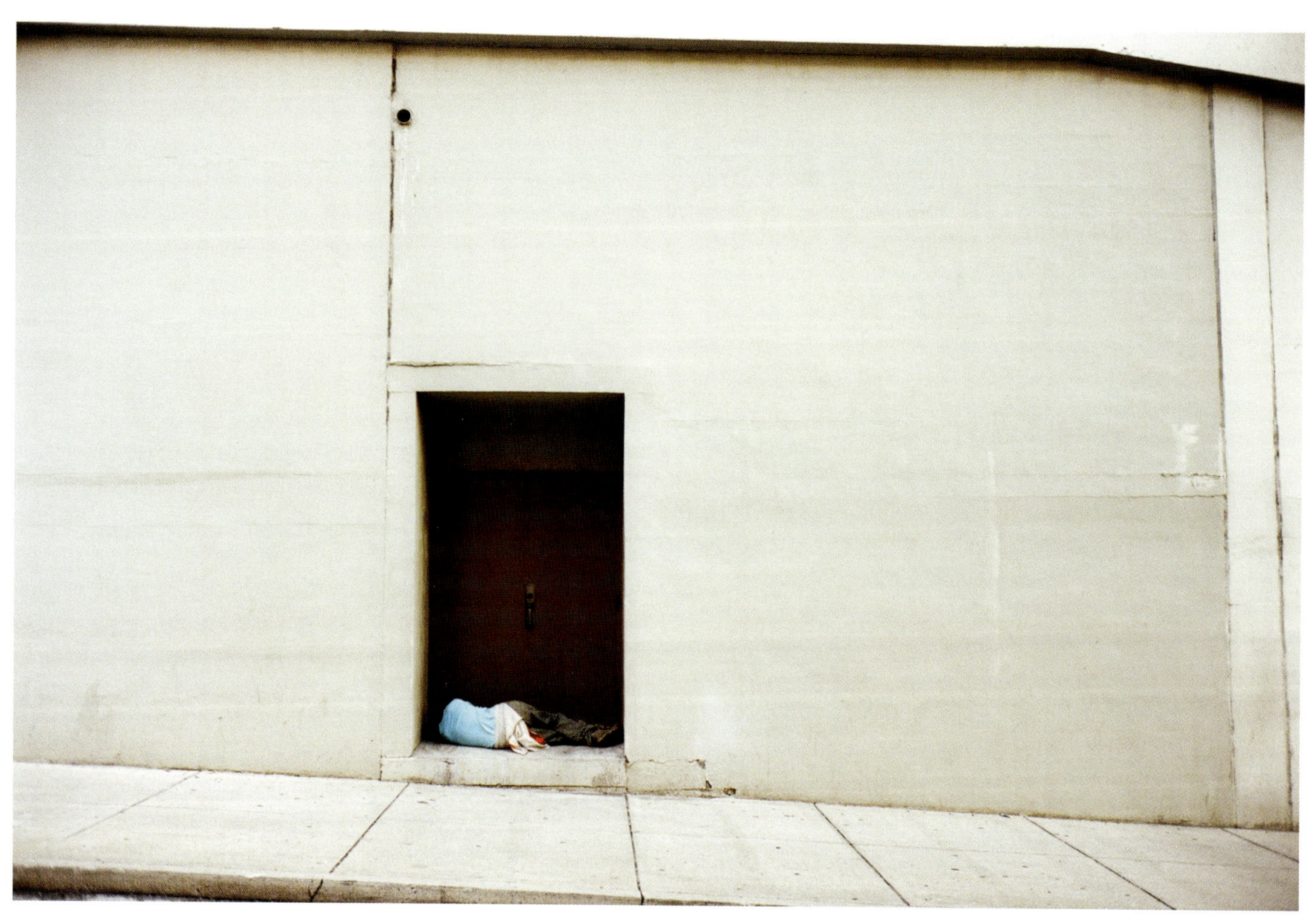

Ray Di Pietro
This Doorway Was His Home, 2018

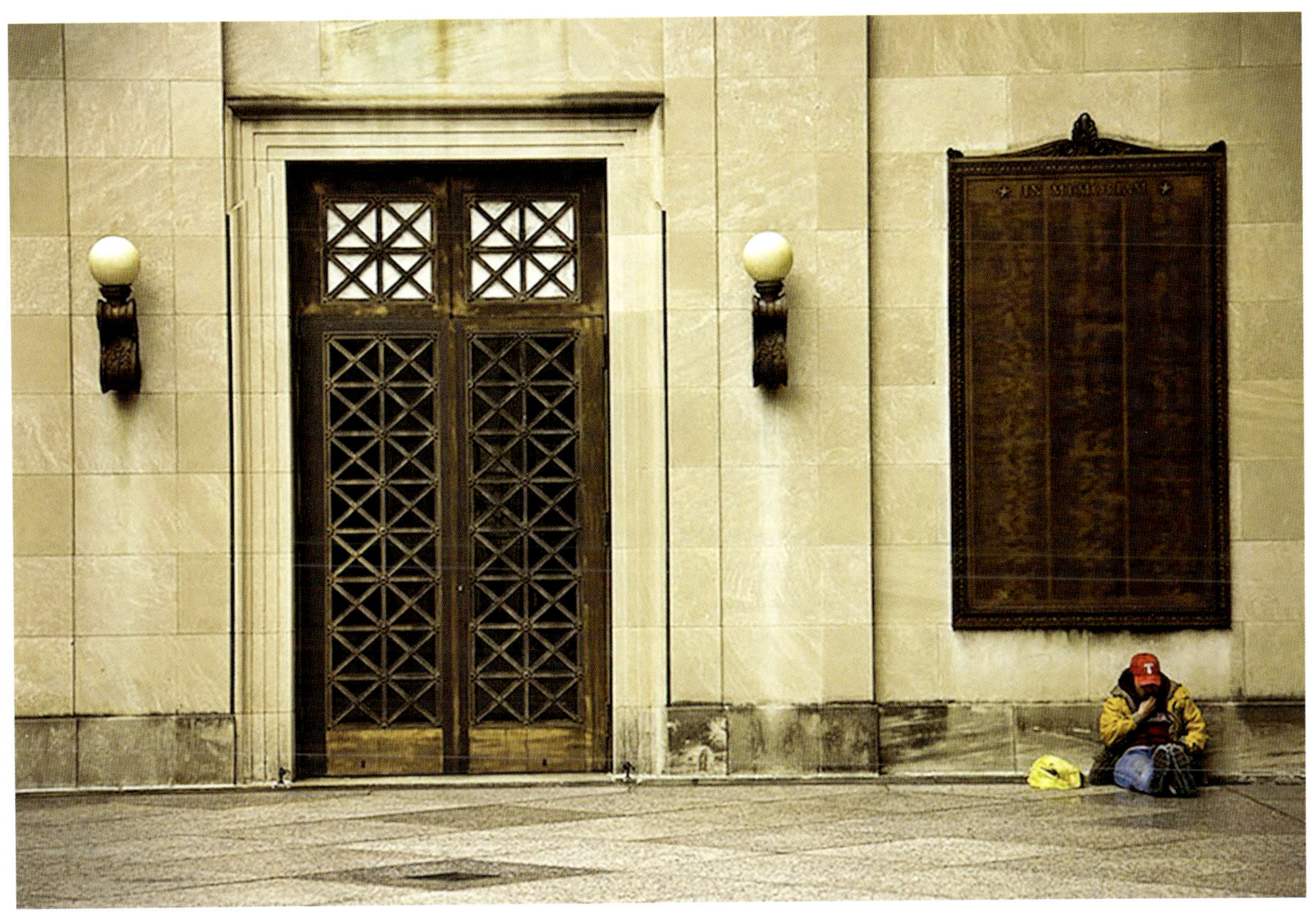

Jacqueline Flynn
Homeless in a Booming City, 2016

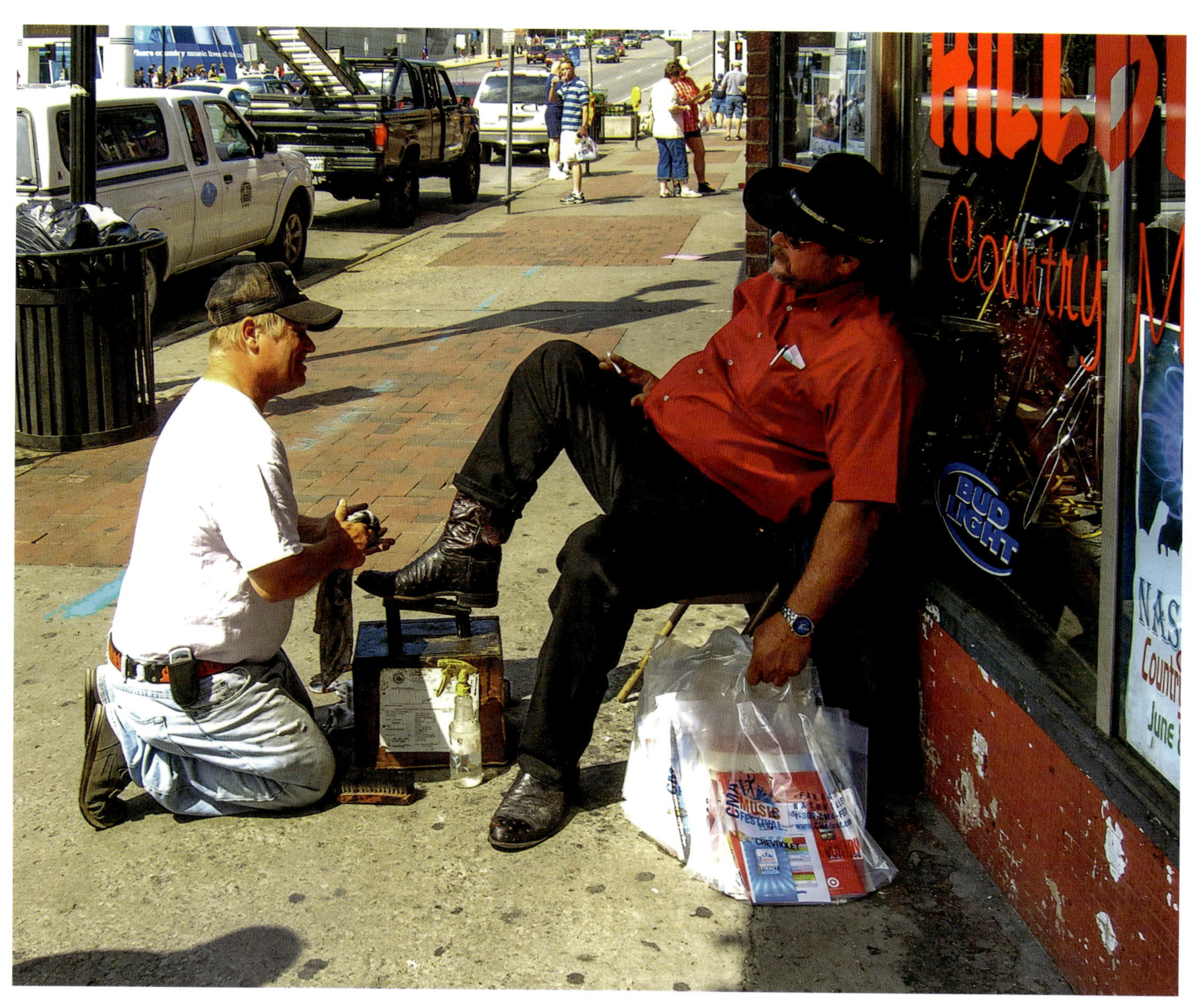

David Bennett
Lower Broadway, 2018

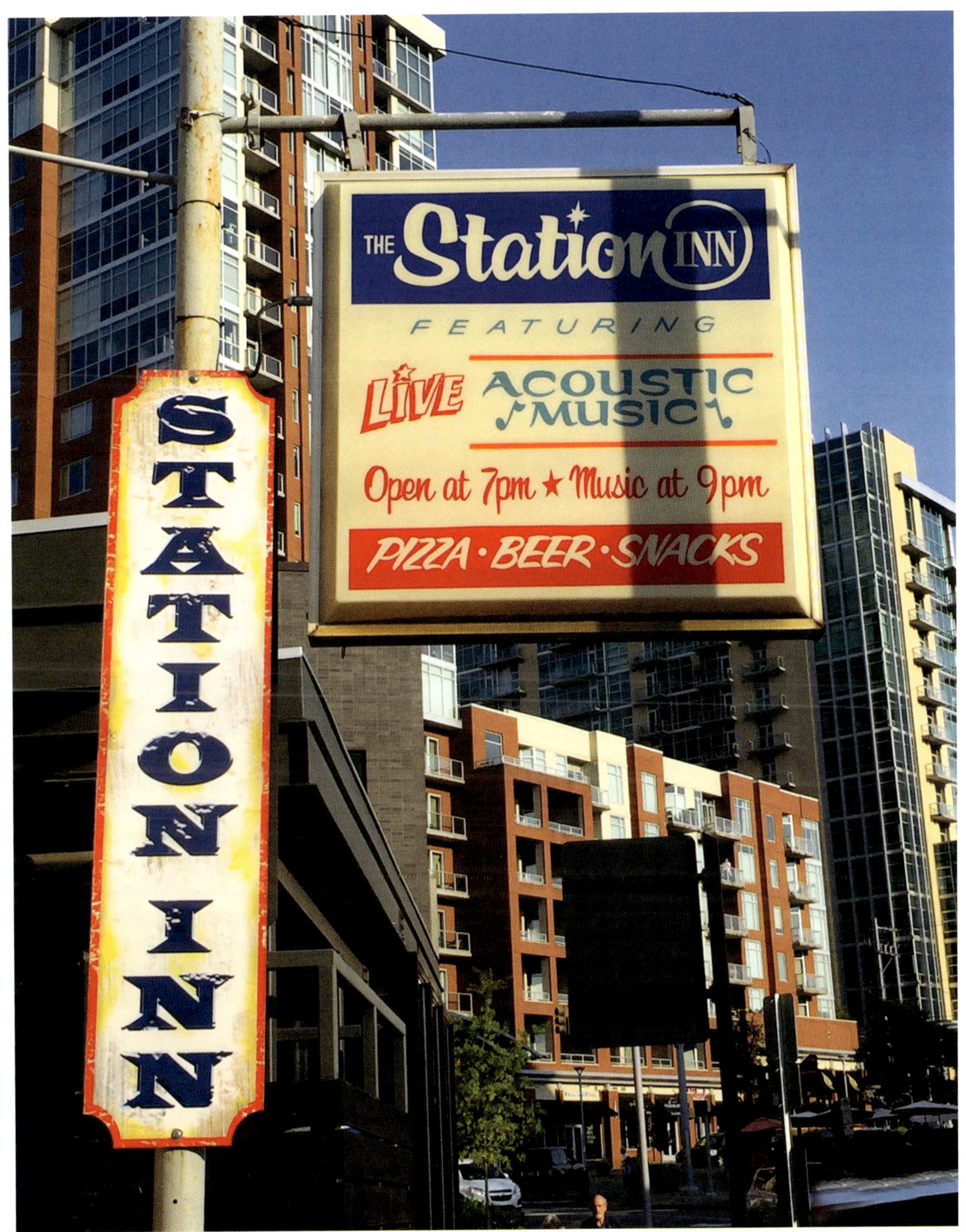

Betty Harper
Grandfathered Inn, 2017

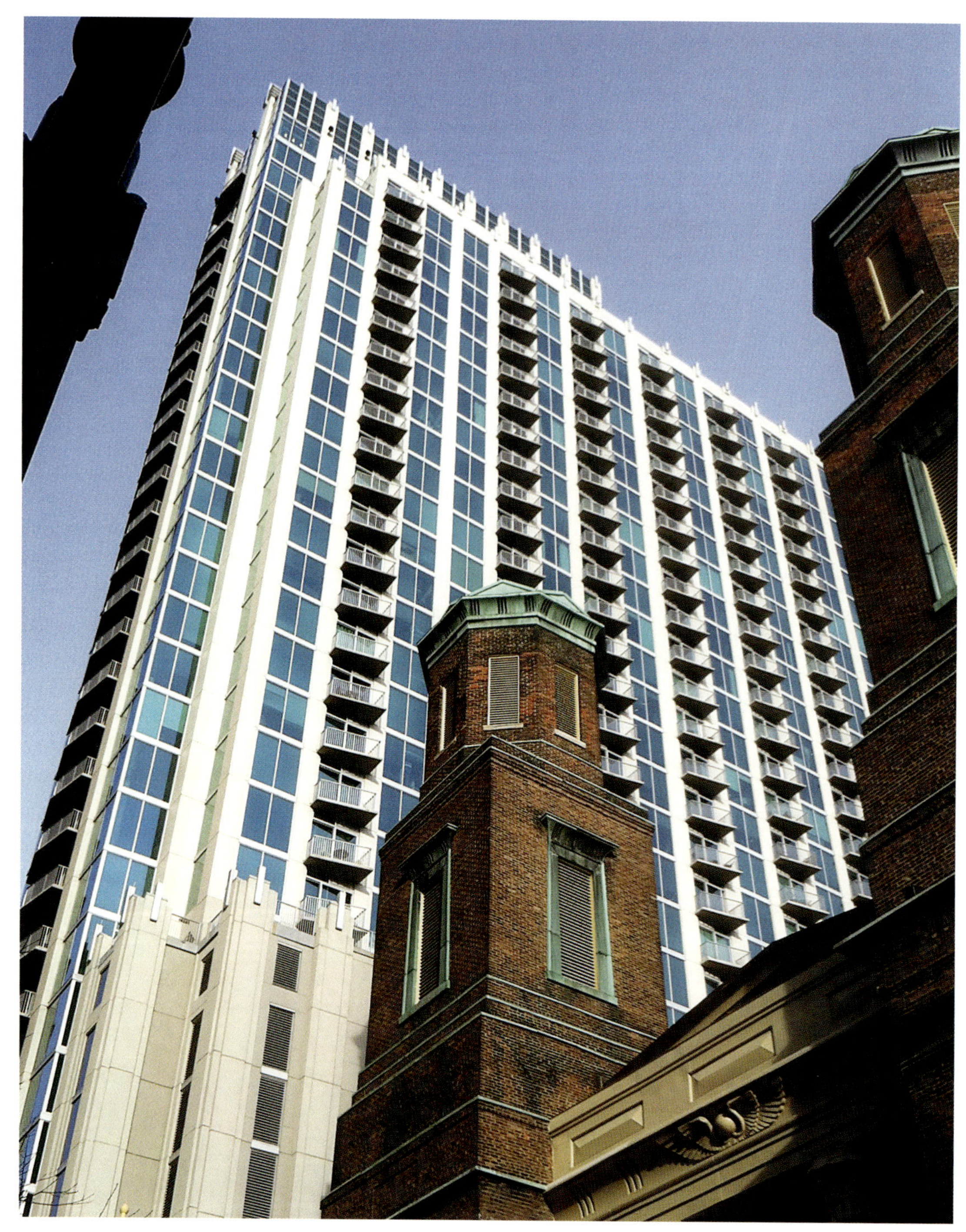

Lisa Sivess Johnson
House of God, 2014

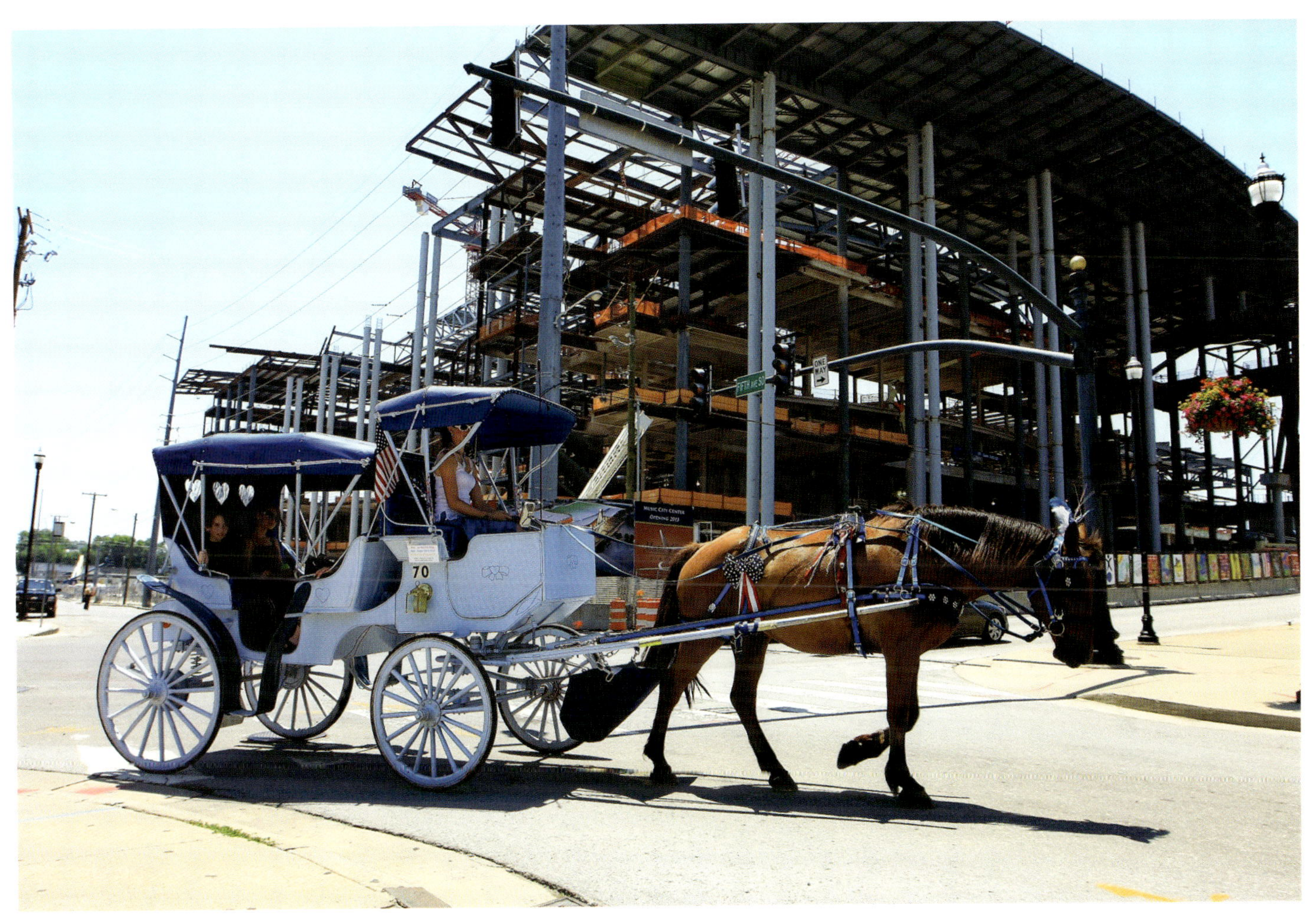

Don McEwen
Music City Center, 2011

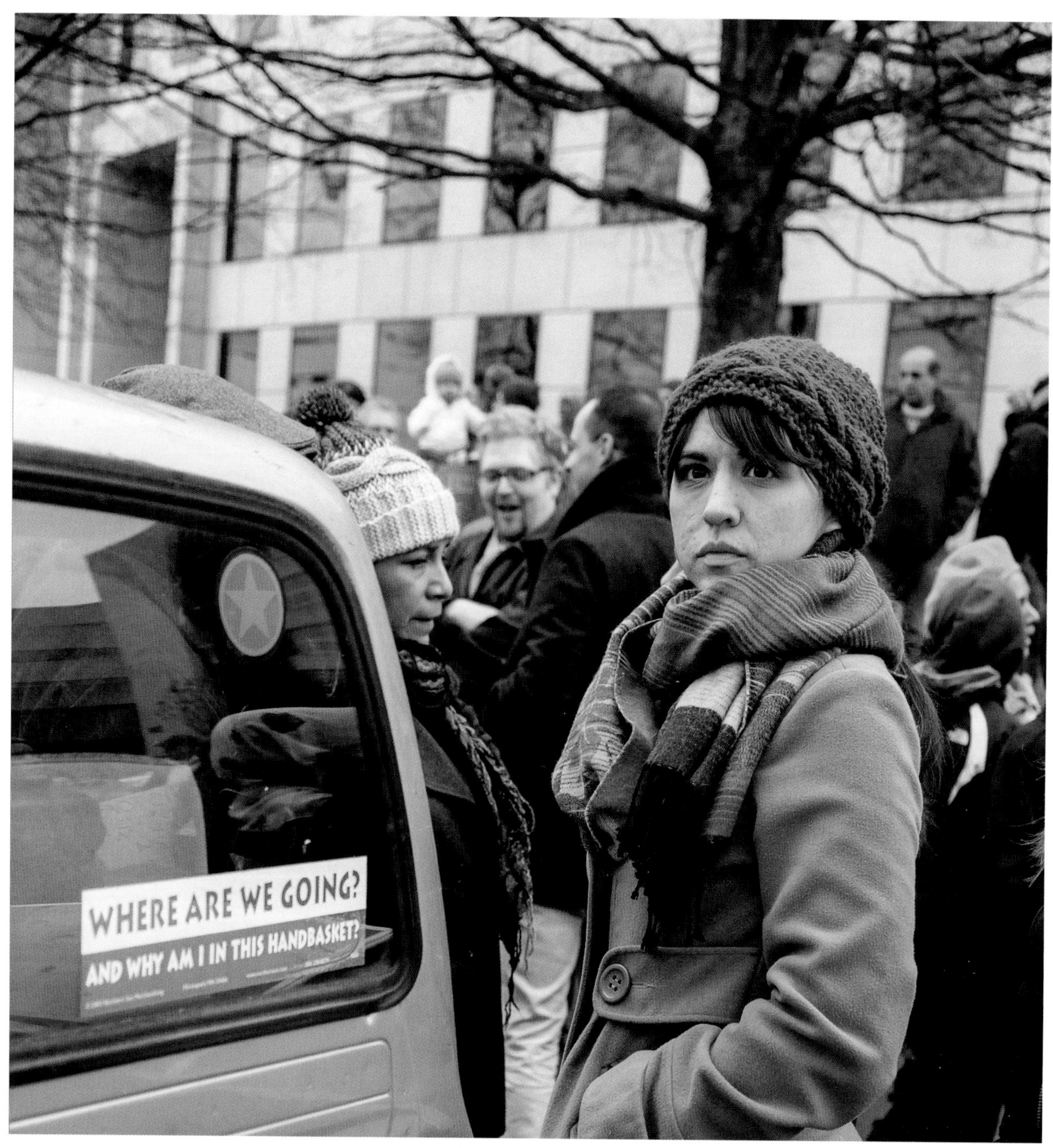

Emily Passino
Where Are We Going, 2017

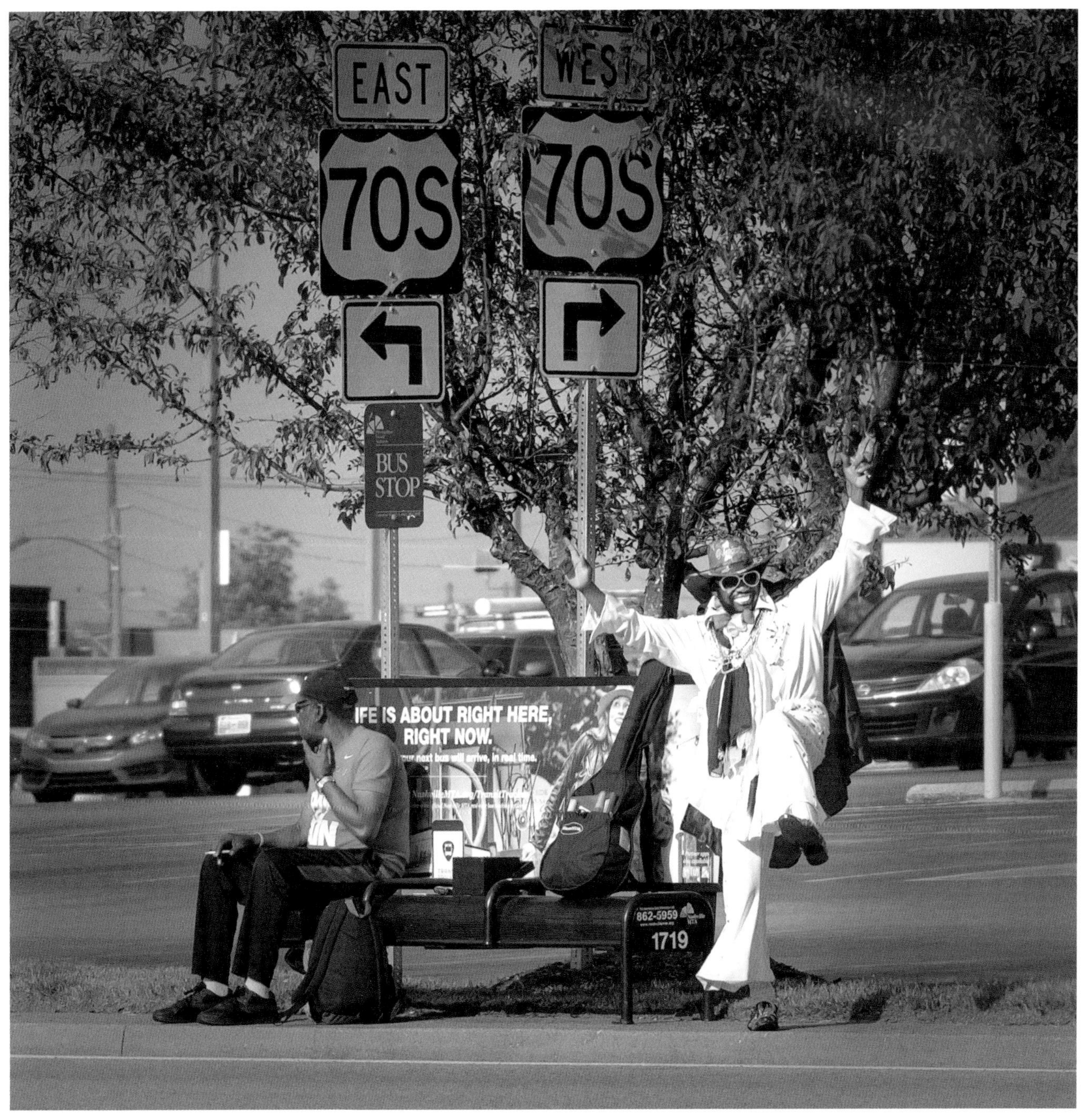

Jo Fields
Life Is . . ., 2018

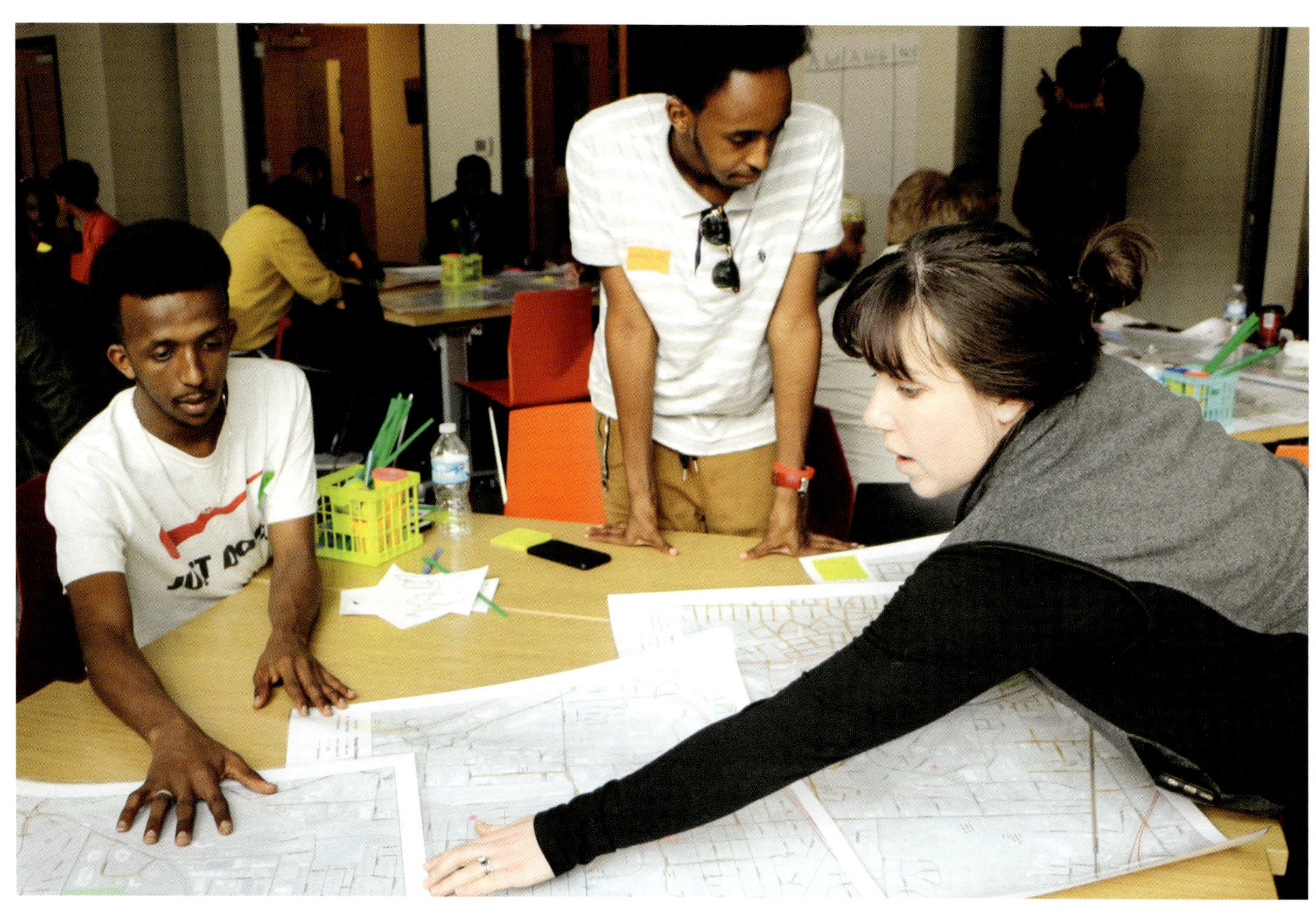

Tony Gonzalez
Visioning, 2016

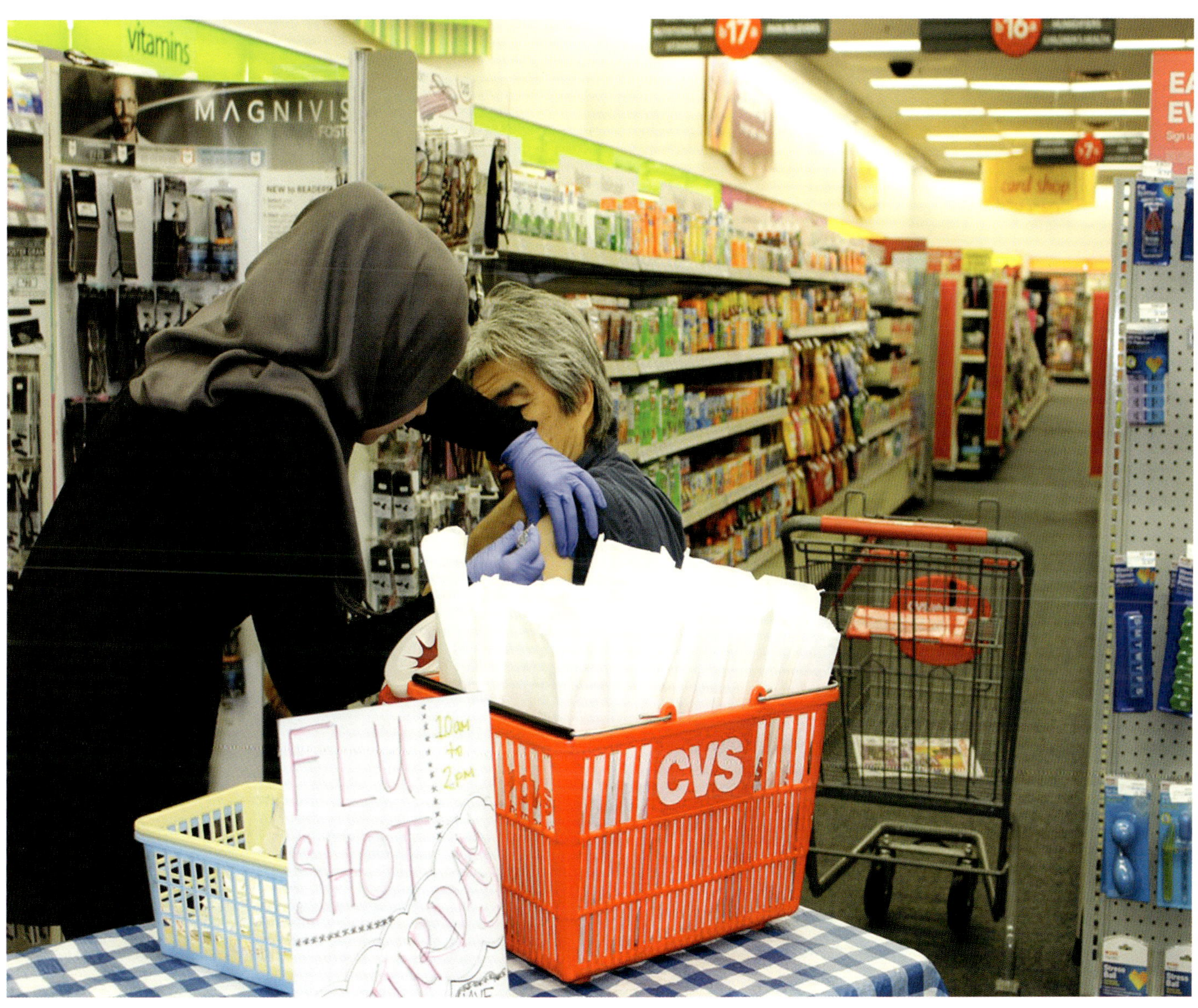

Yukiko Ueda
Free Flu Shot, 2017

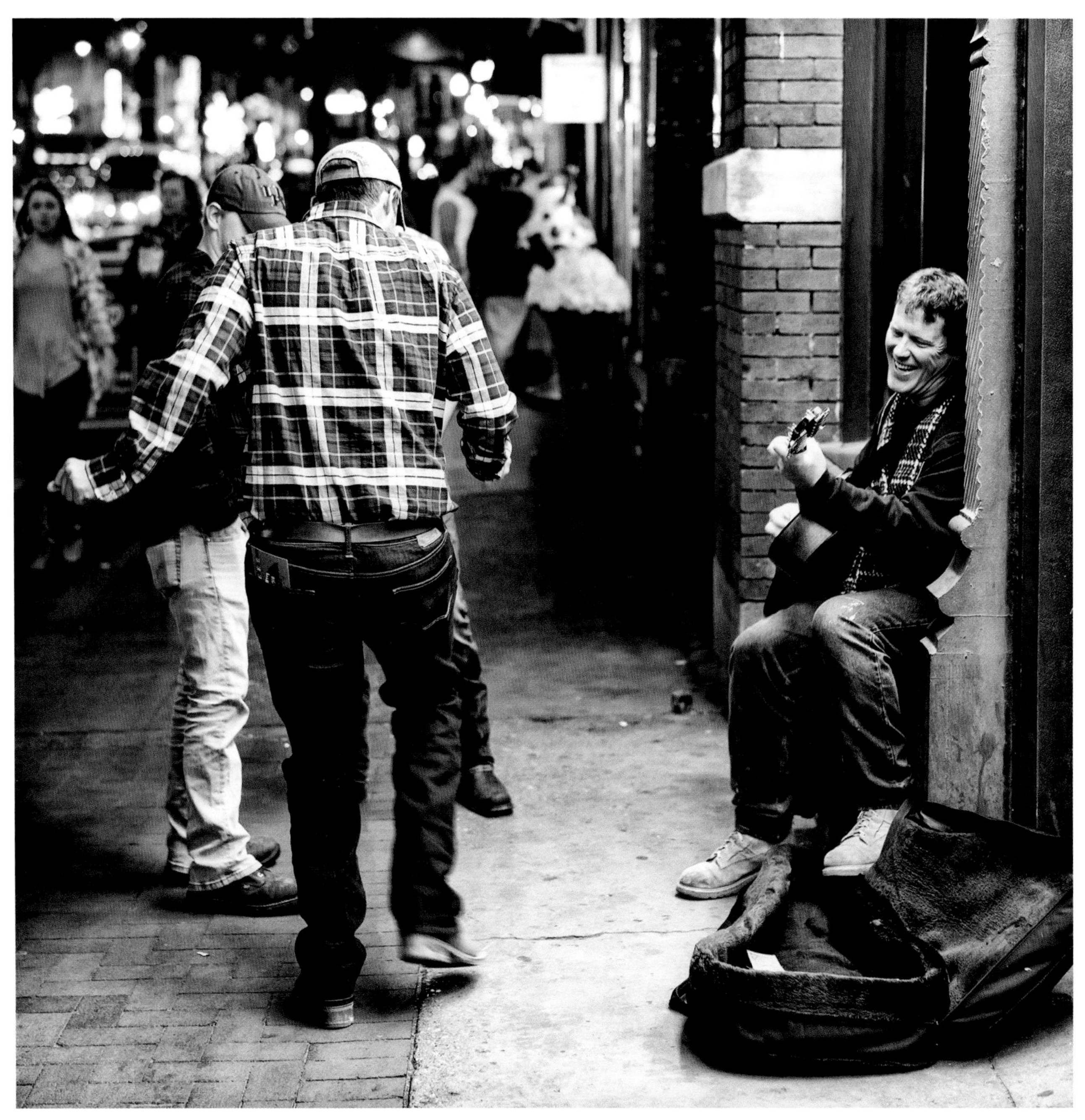

David Morel
When the Music Moves You, 2016

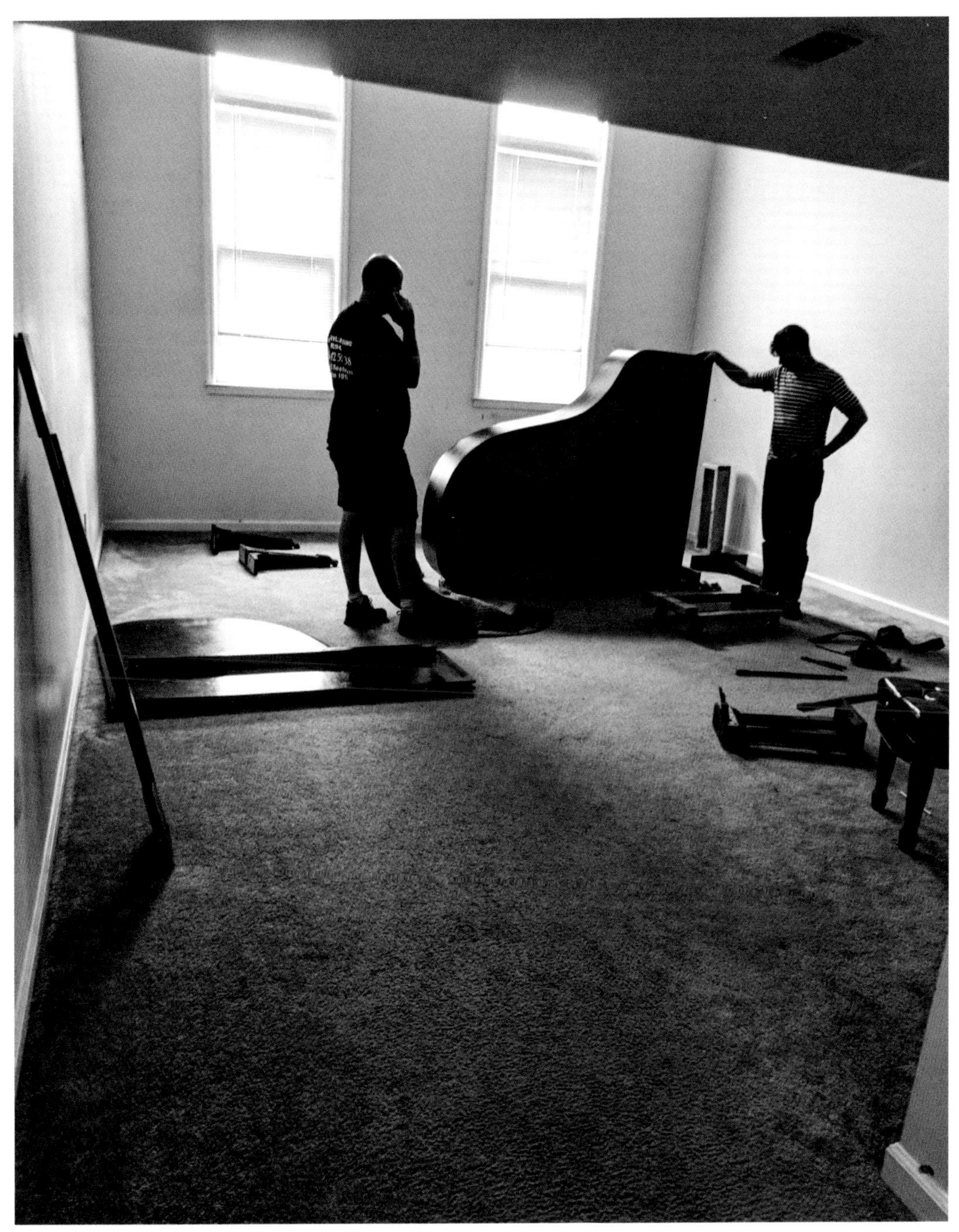

Justin Near
Piano Moving, 2018

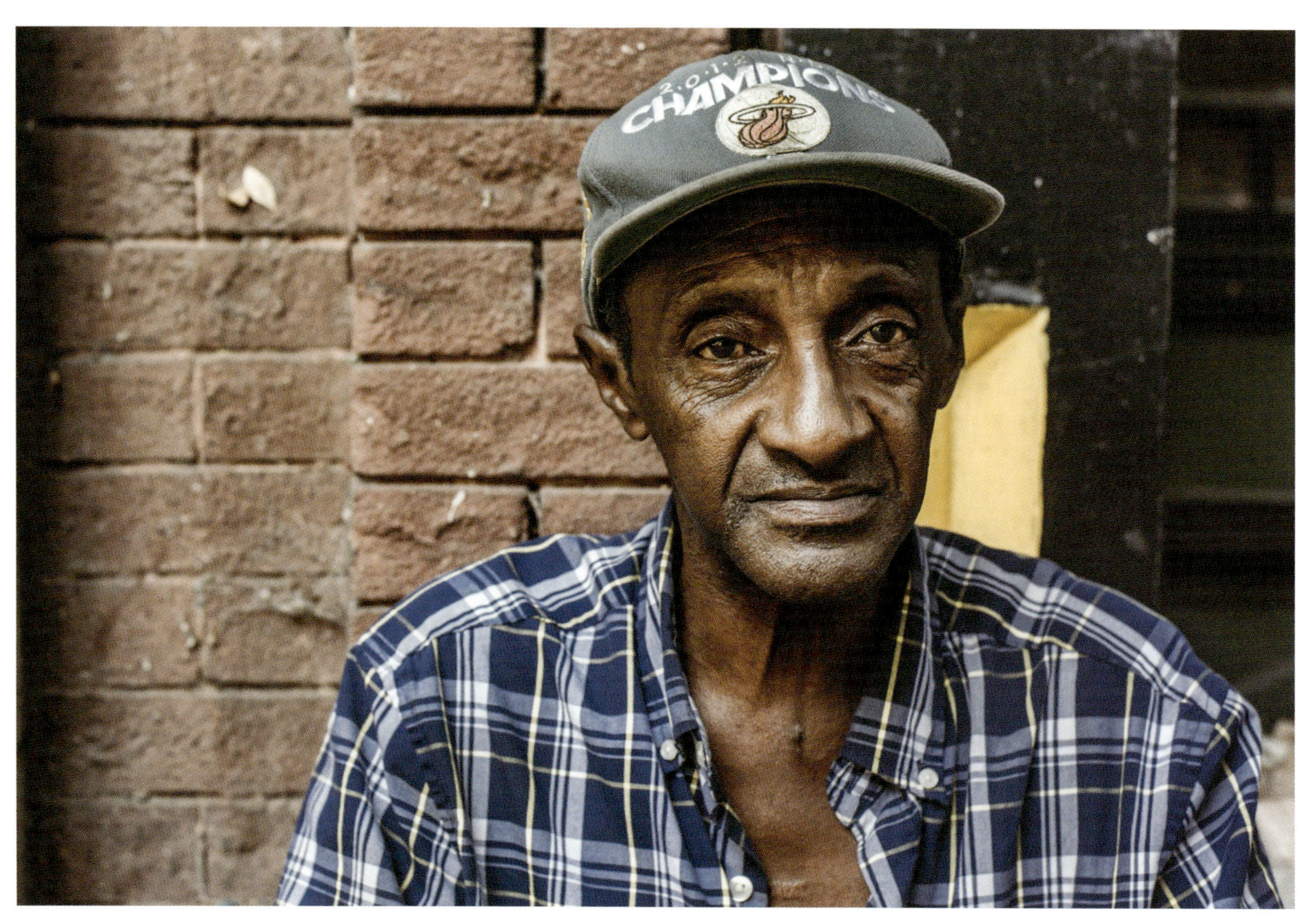

Nick Zimmer
Disconnect, 2016

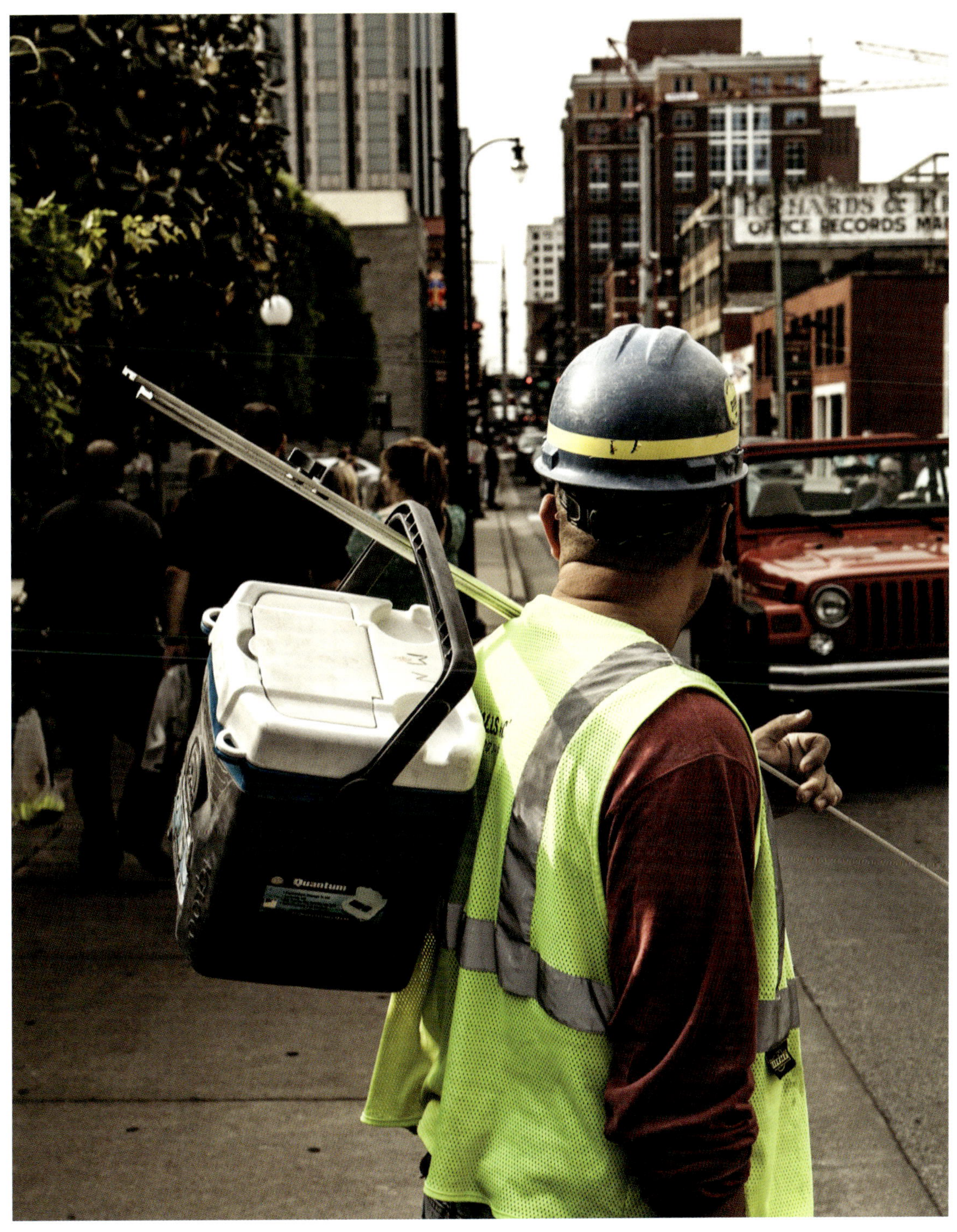

DaShawn Lewis
Common Practices, 2018

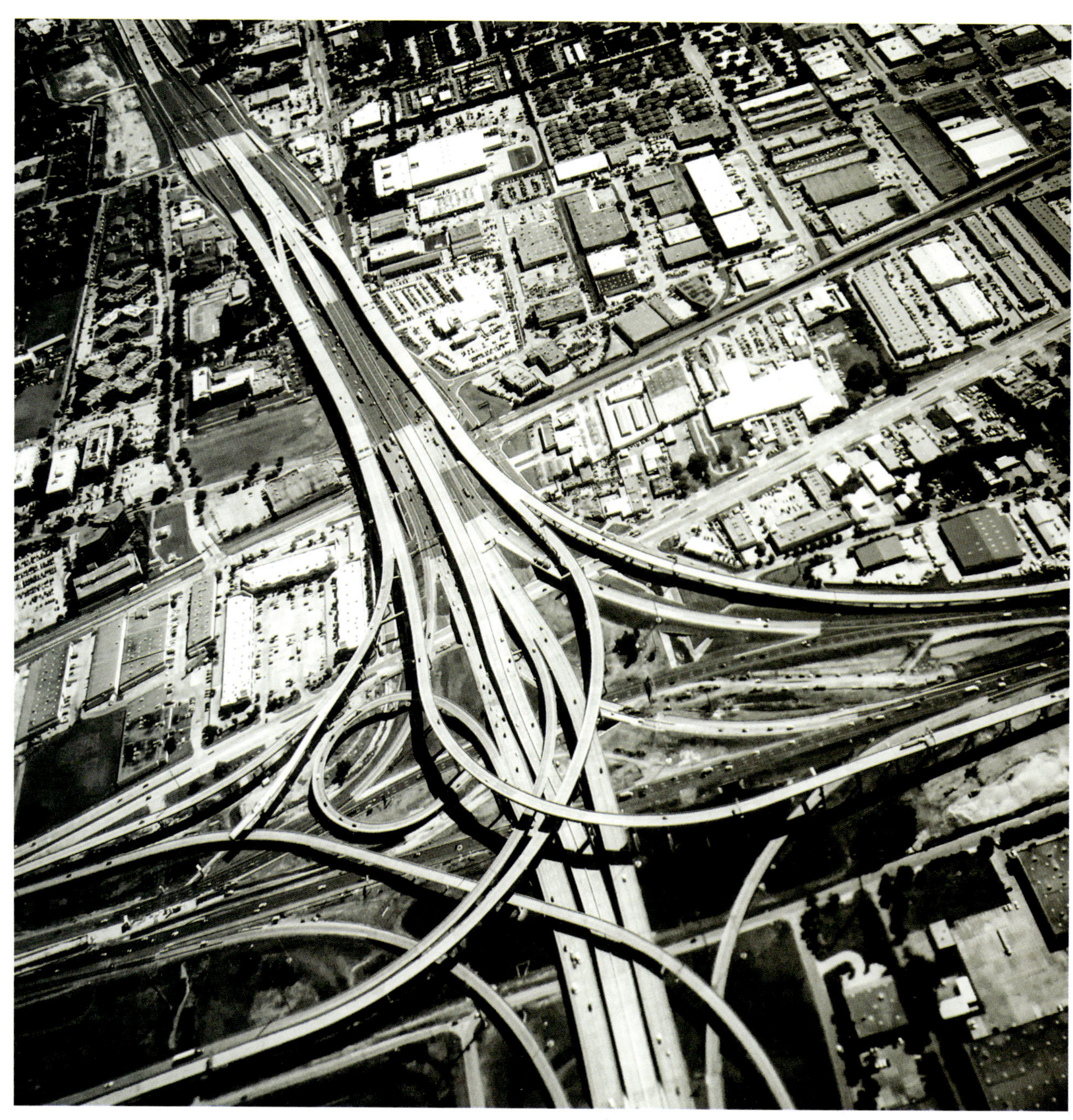

Kim Balevre
Spaghetti Junction, 2016

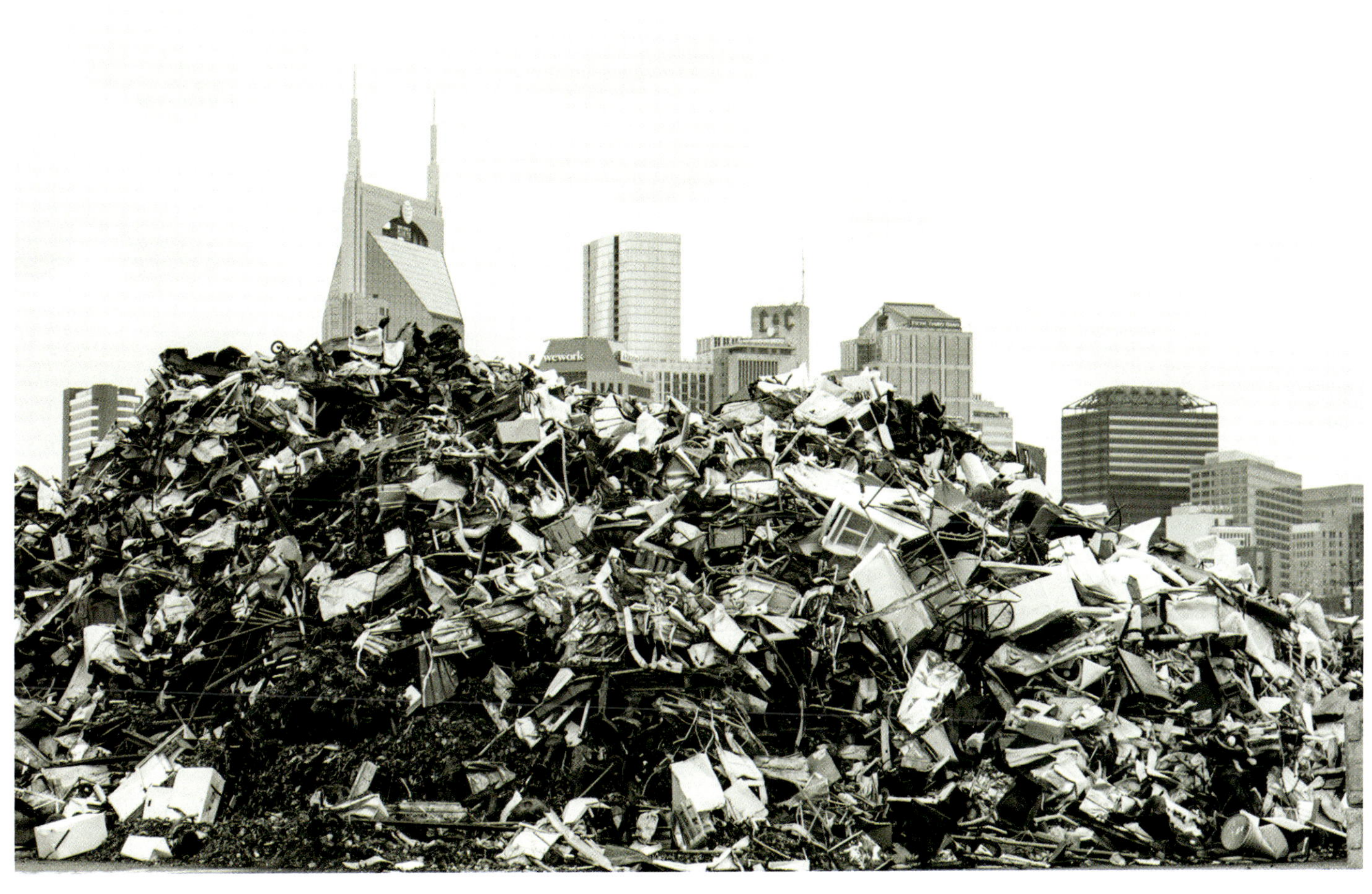

David Piñeros

Under the Music City, 2018

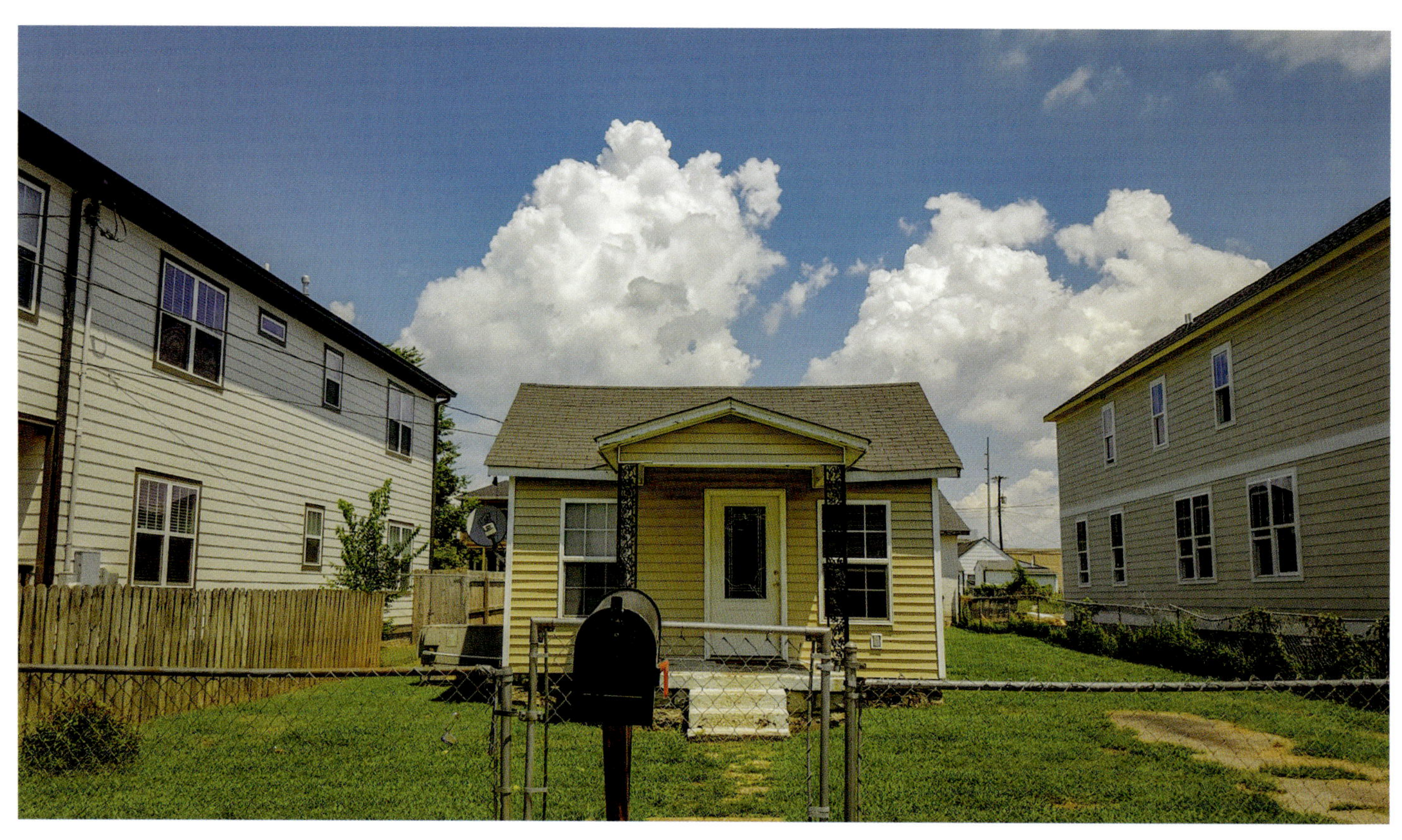

Brian Siskind
The Nations Life, 2016

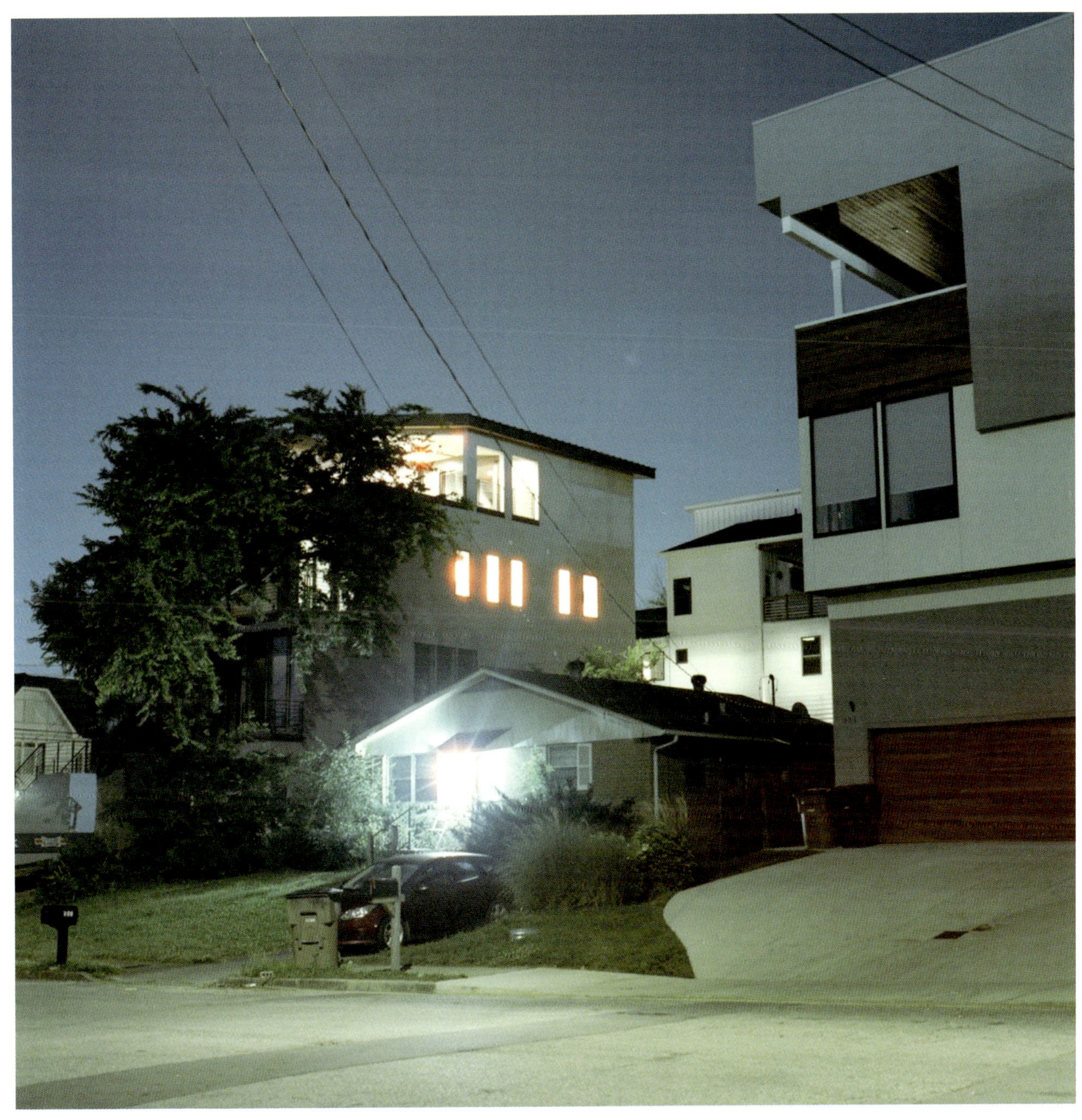

Erik Doty
New Neighbors, 2018

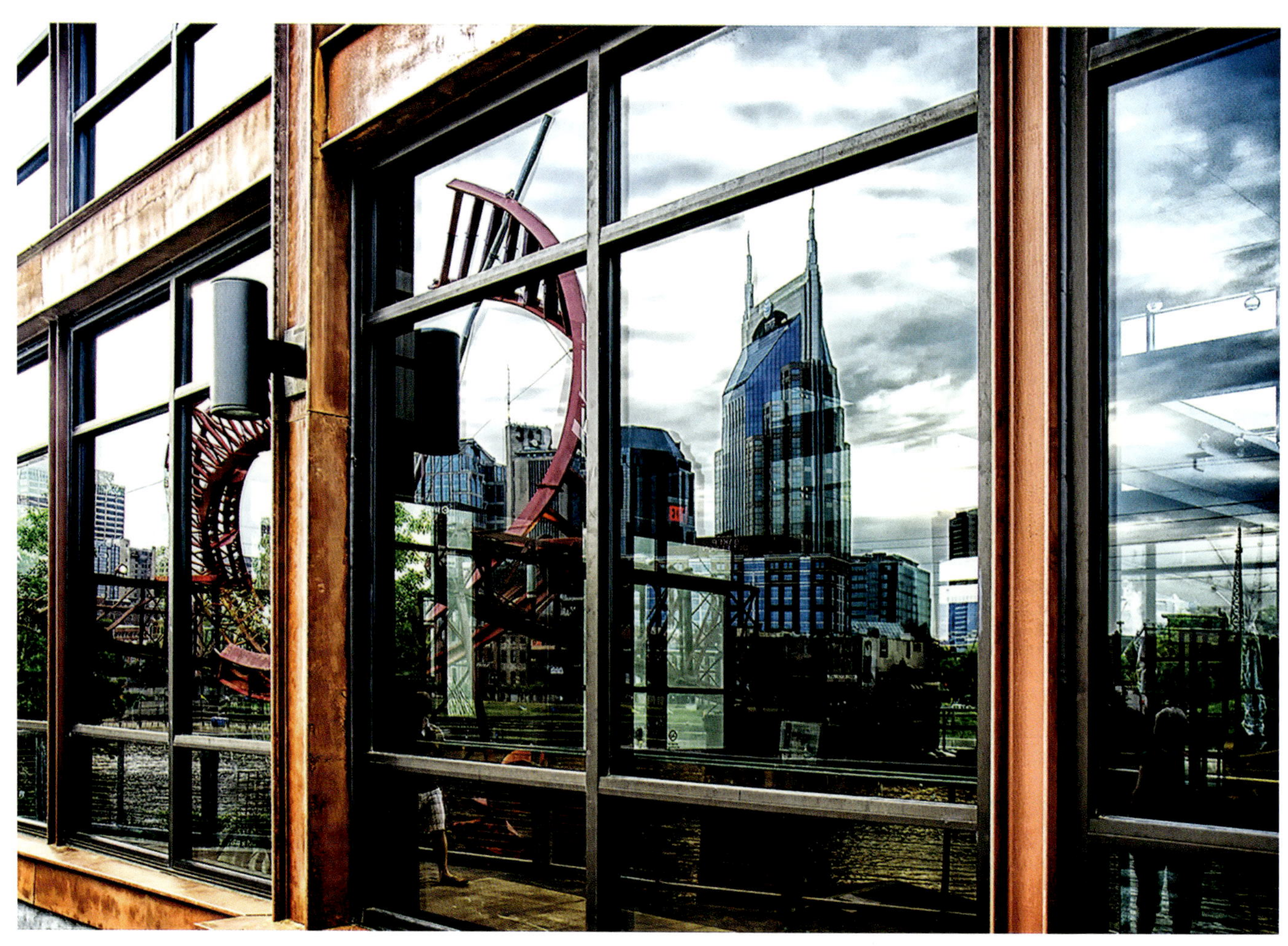

John Roeder
Nashville Skyline East View, 2013

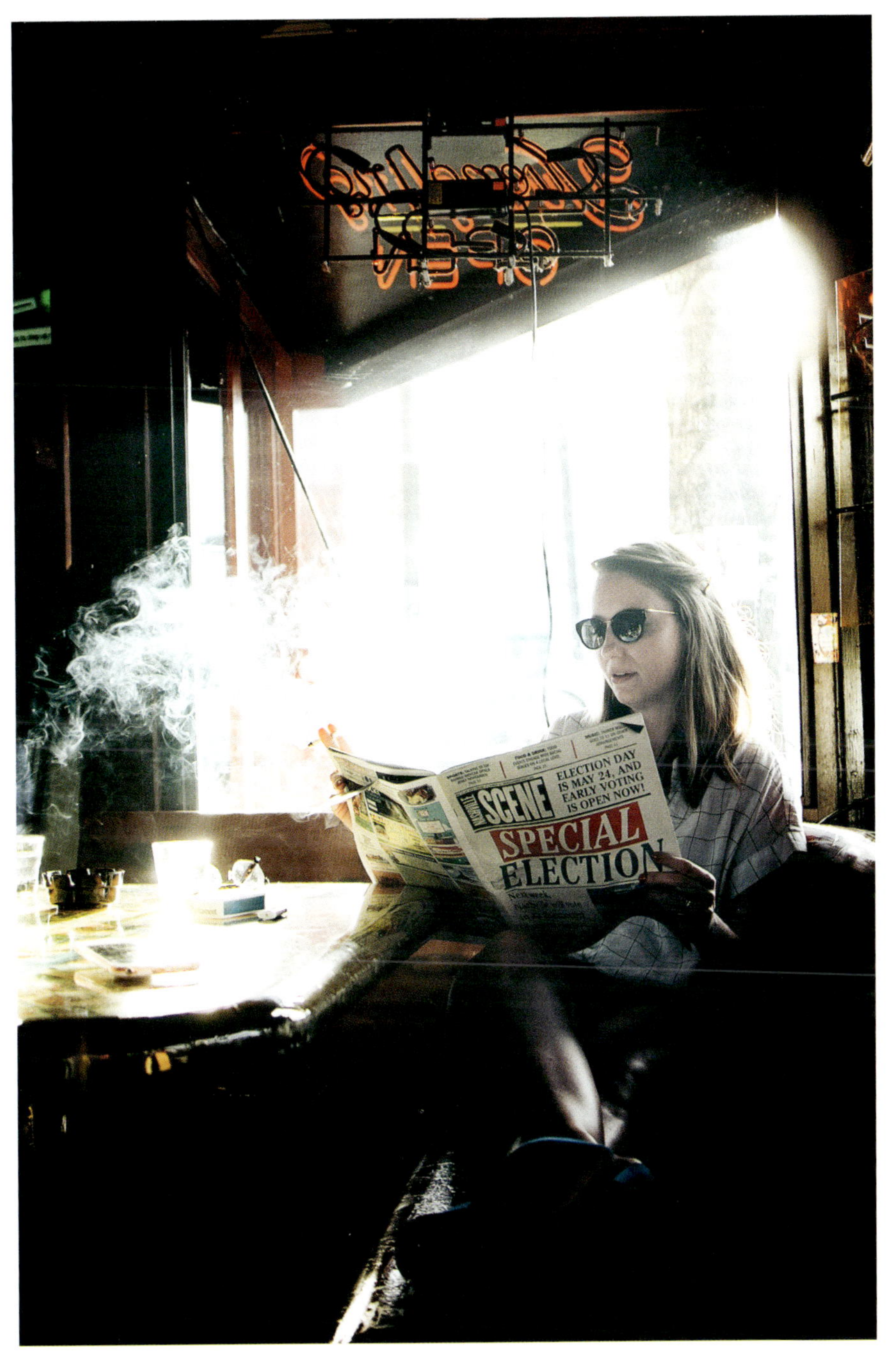

Julia Lynn Perkins
Extra, Extra, 2018

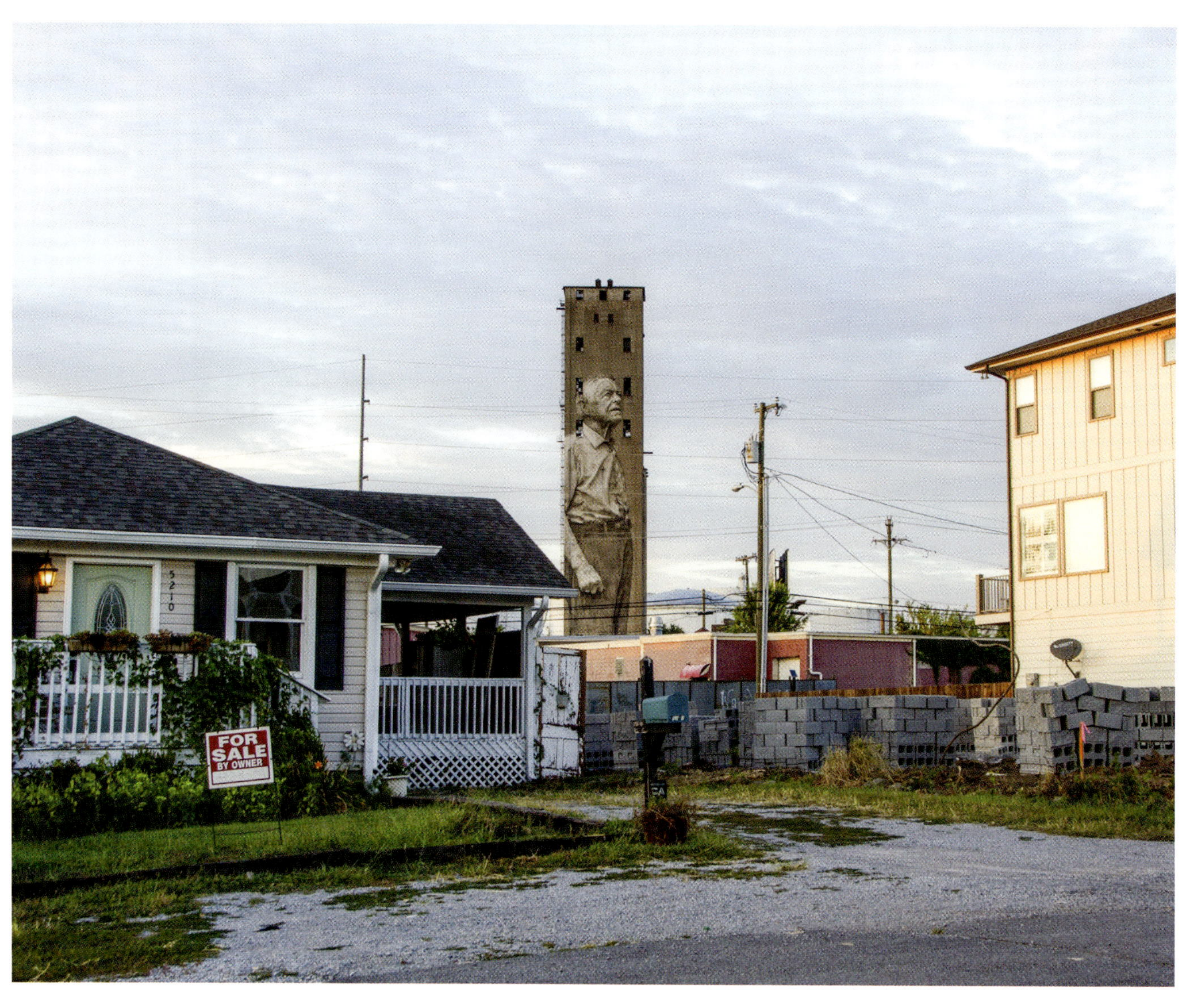

Elizabeth Berger
Mr. Estes Ponders Progress, 2018

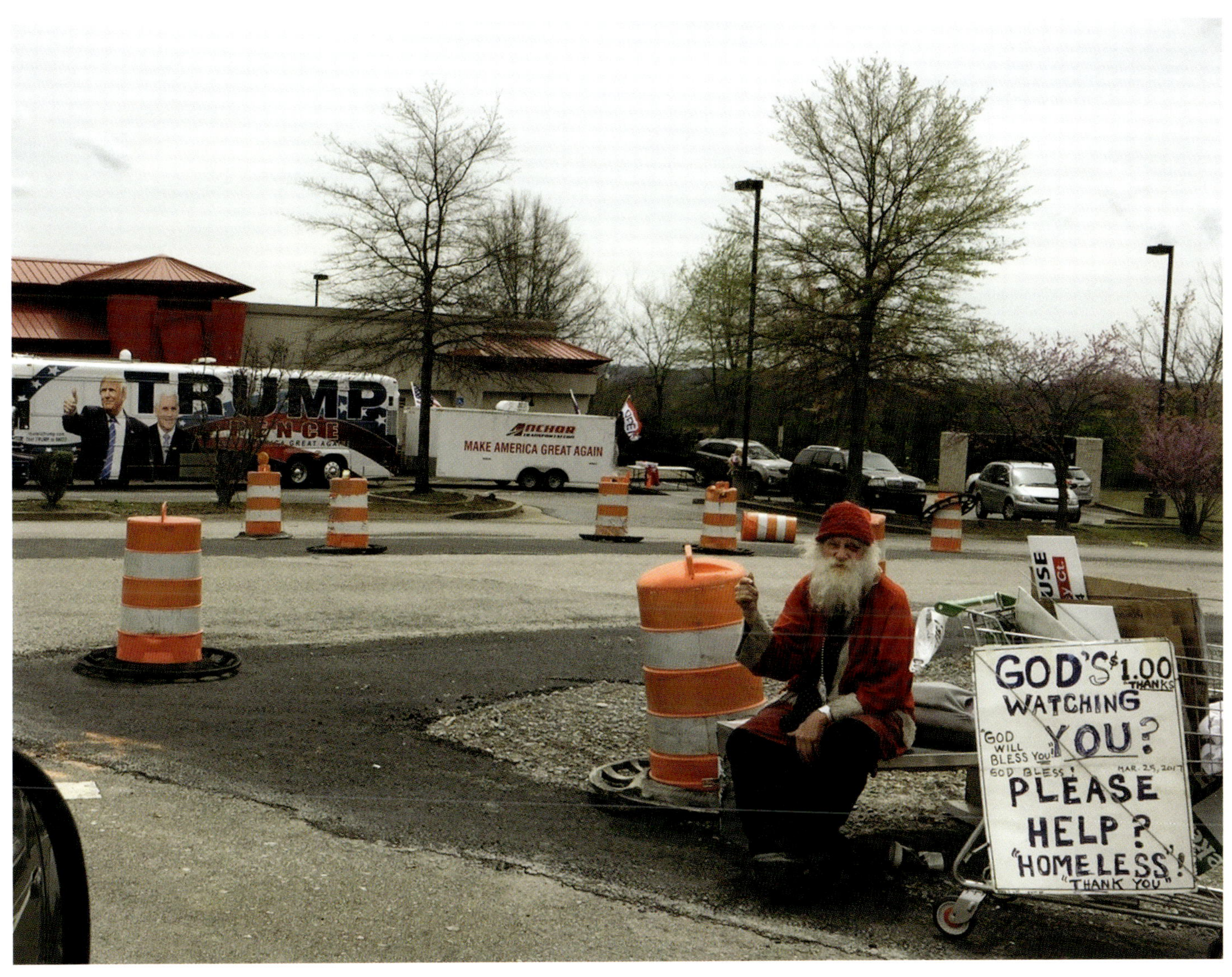

Martha Armstrong
Make Bellevue Great Again, 2017

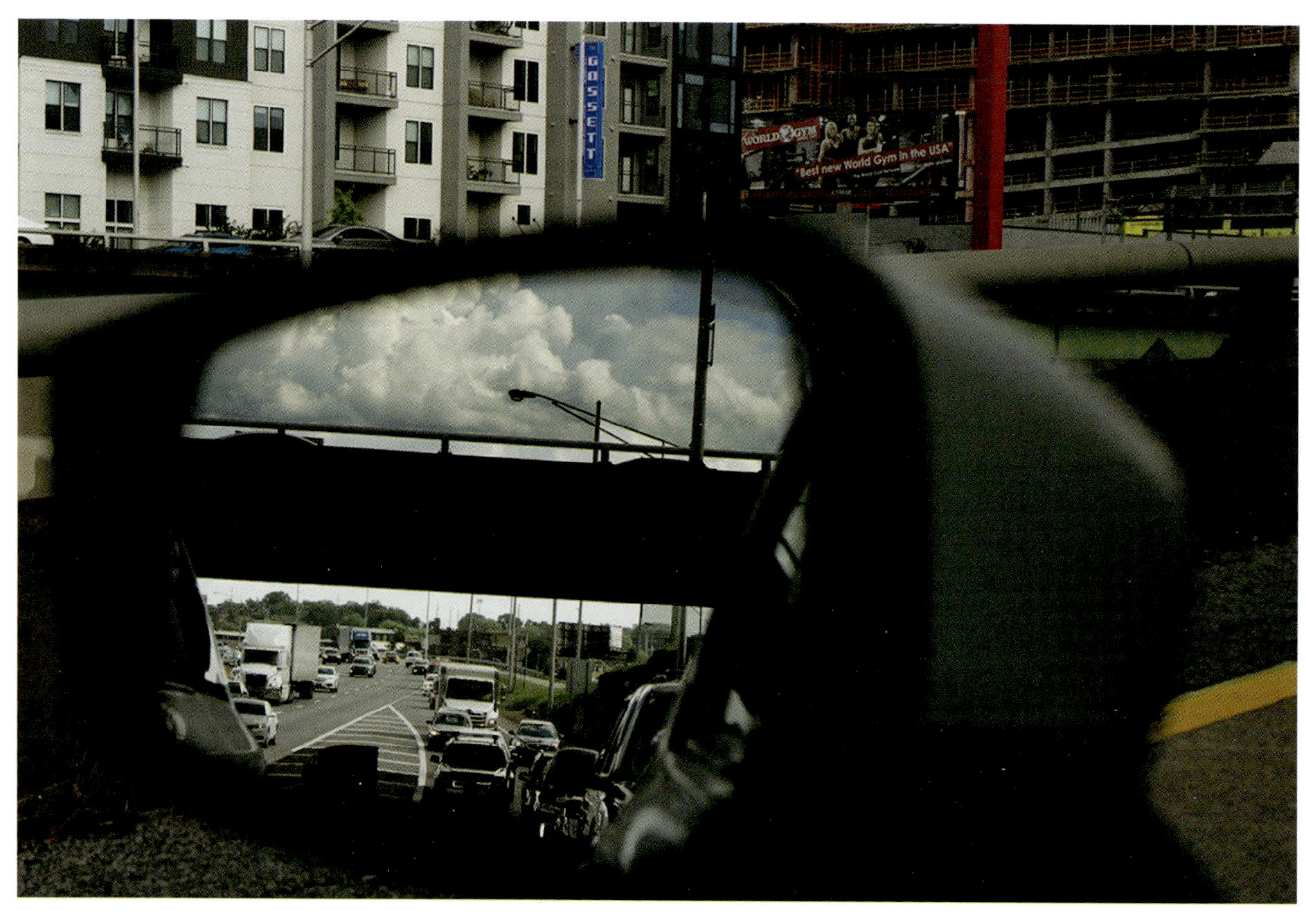

Ramona Wiggins
Growing Pains in the "It City," 2018

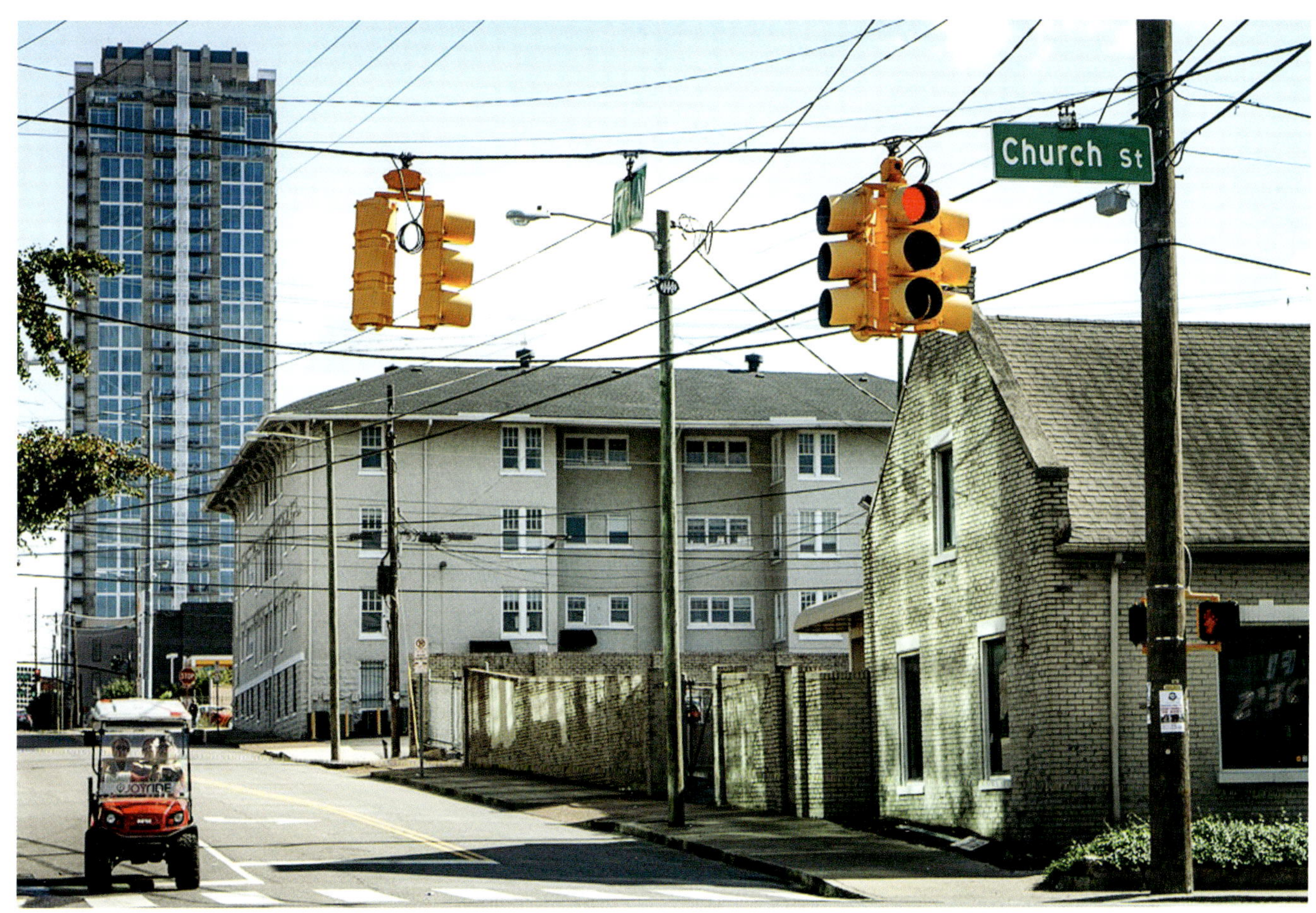

Mary Phelps
17th & Church, 2018

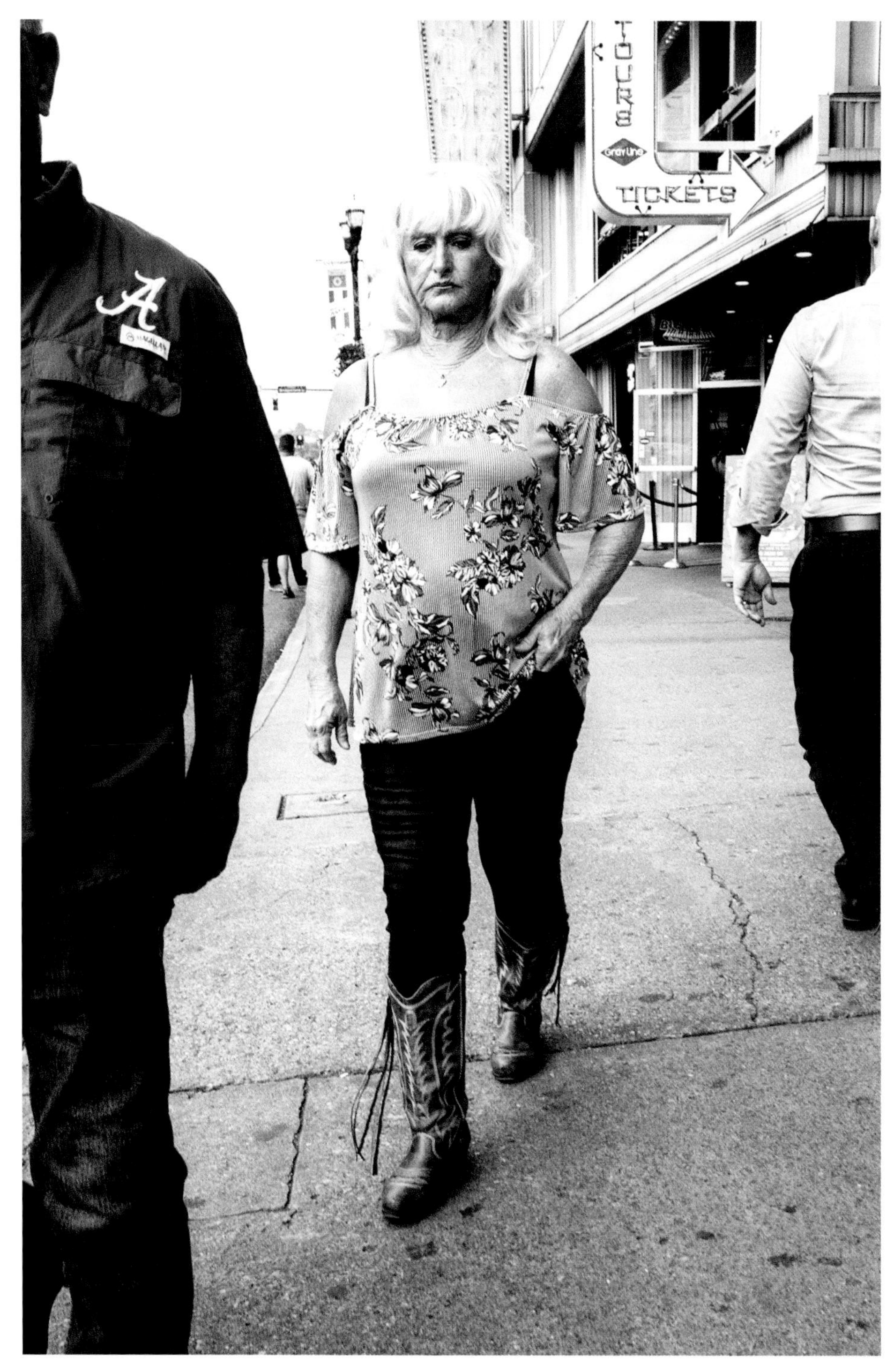

Huy Nguyen
Uncertainty, 2018

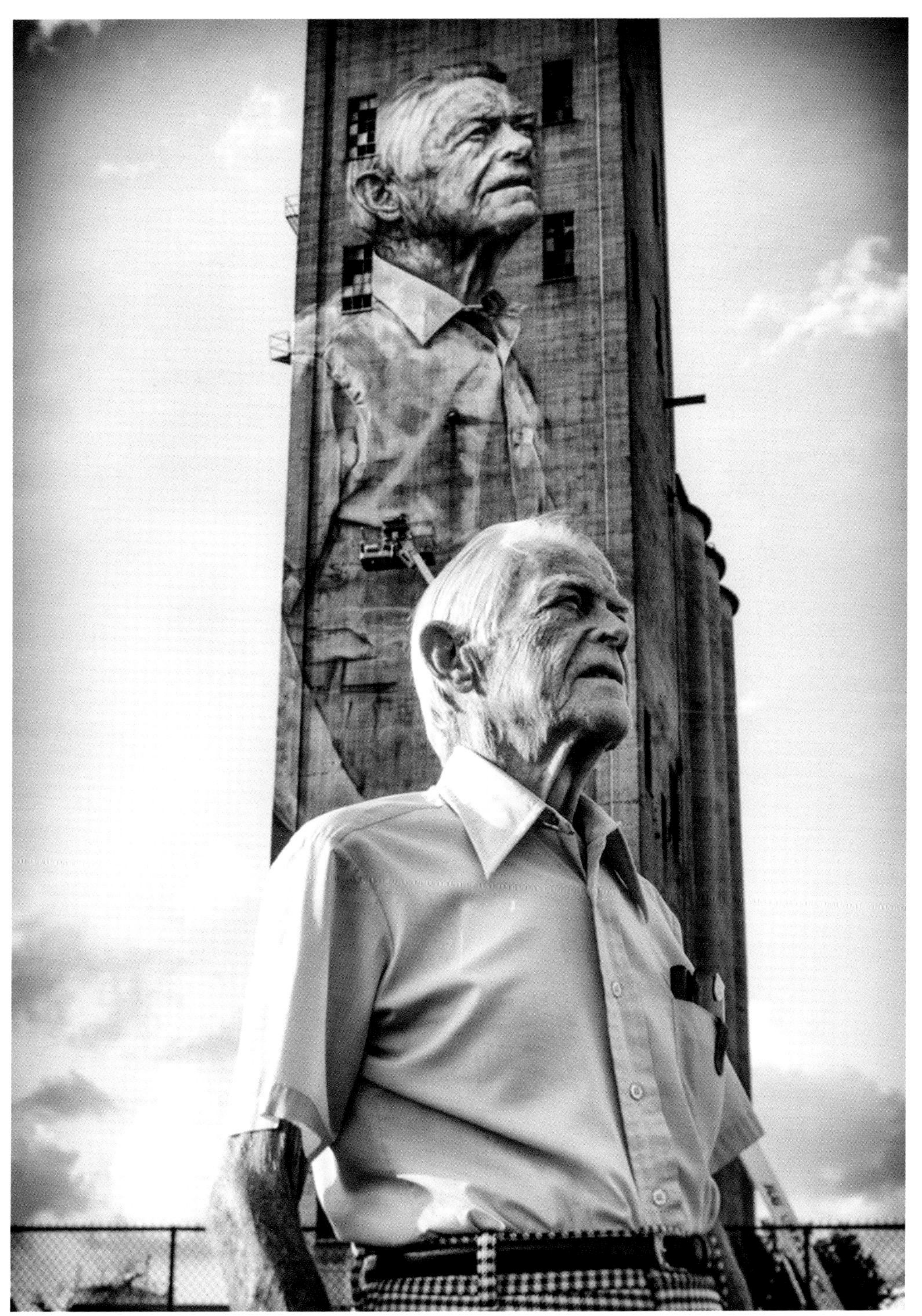

James DeMain
Mr. Estes, 2018

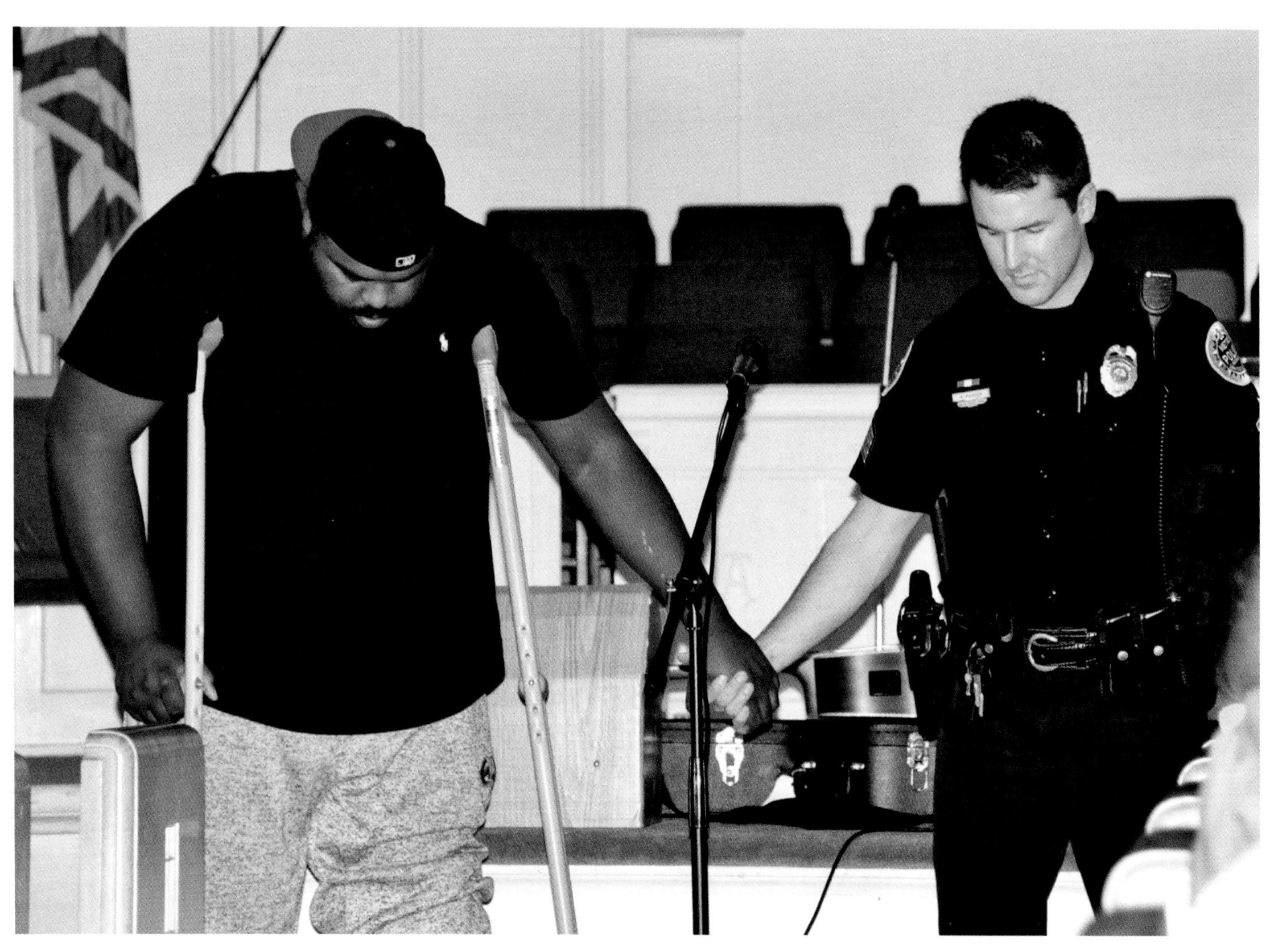

Donna Moffitt
Rise Above, 2016

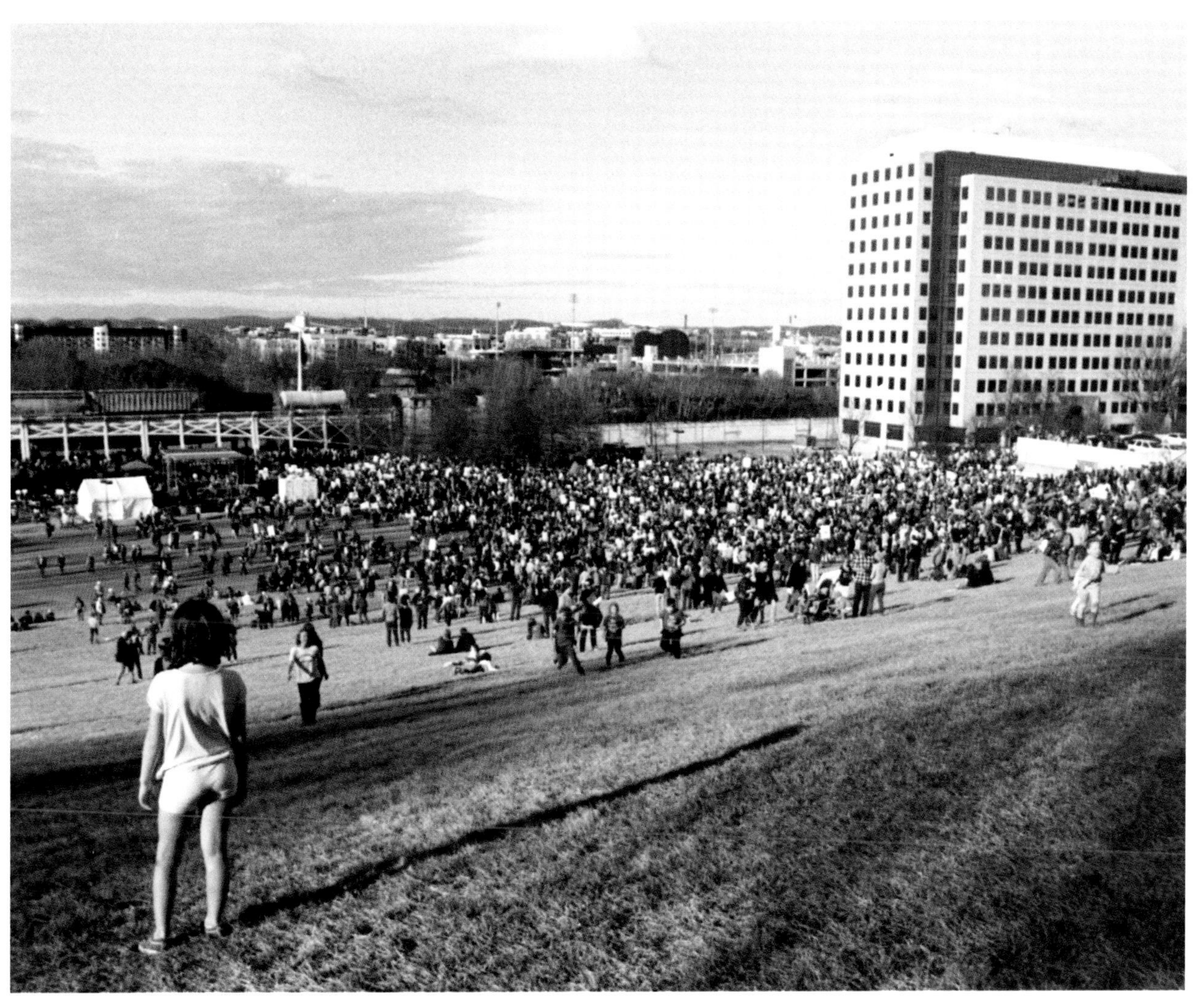

Hamilton Masters
Future, 2018

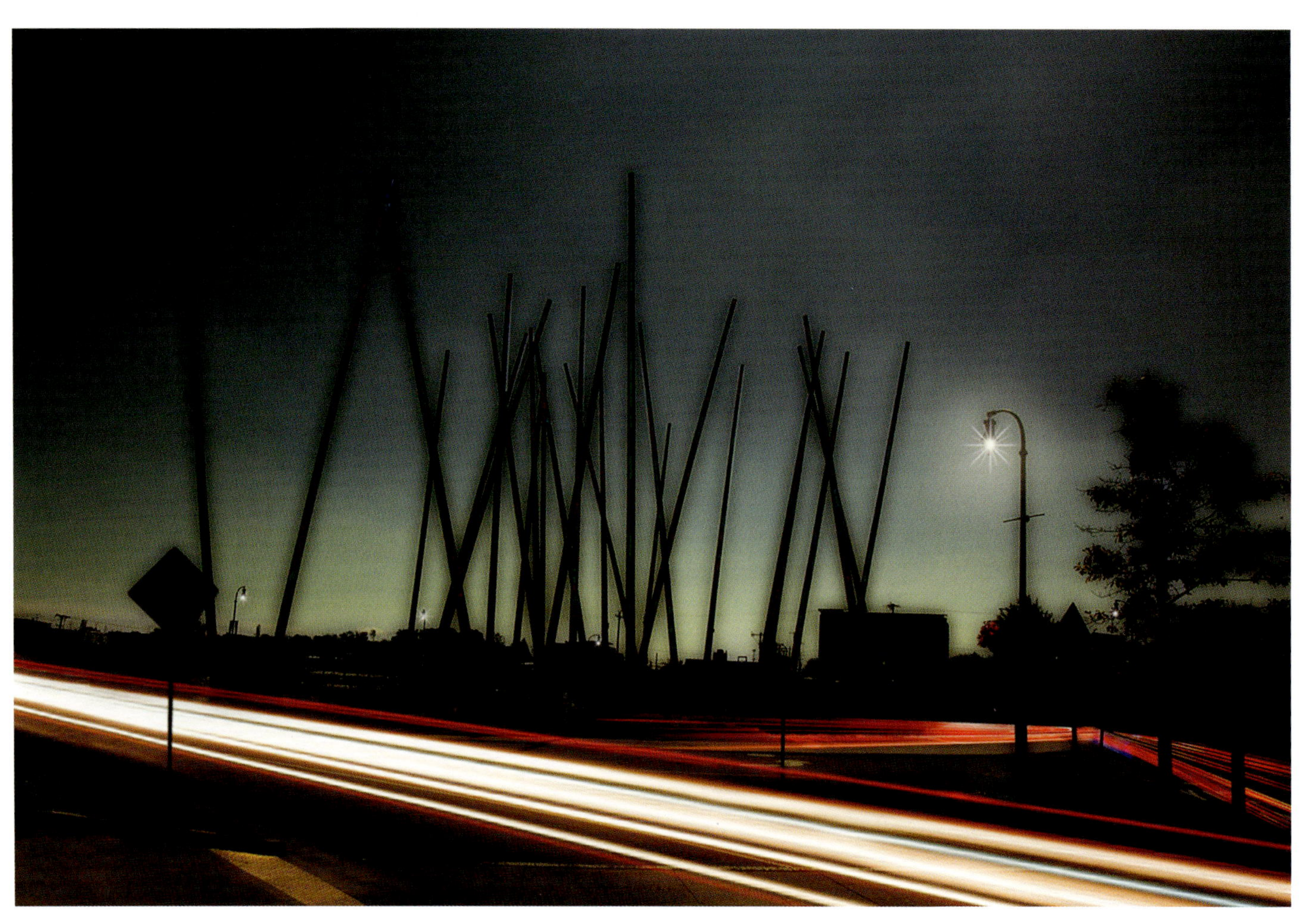

Ben Spalding
Nashville Stix Roundabout, 2018

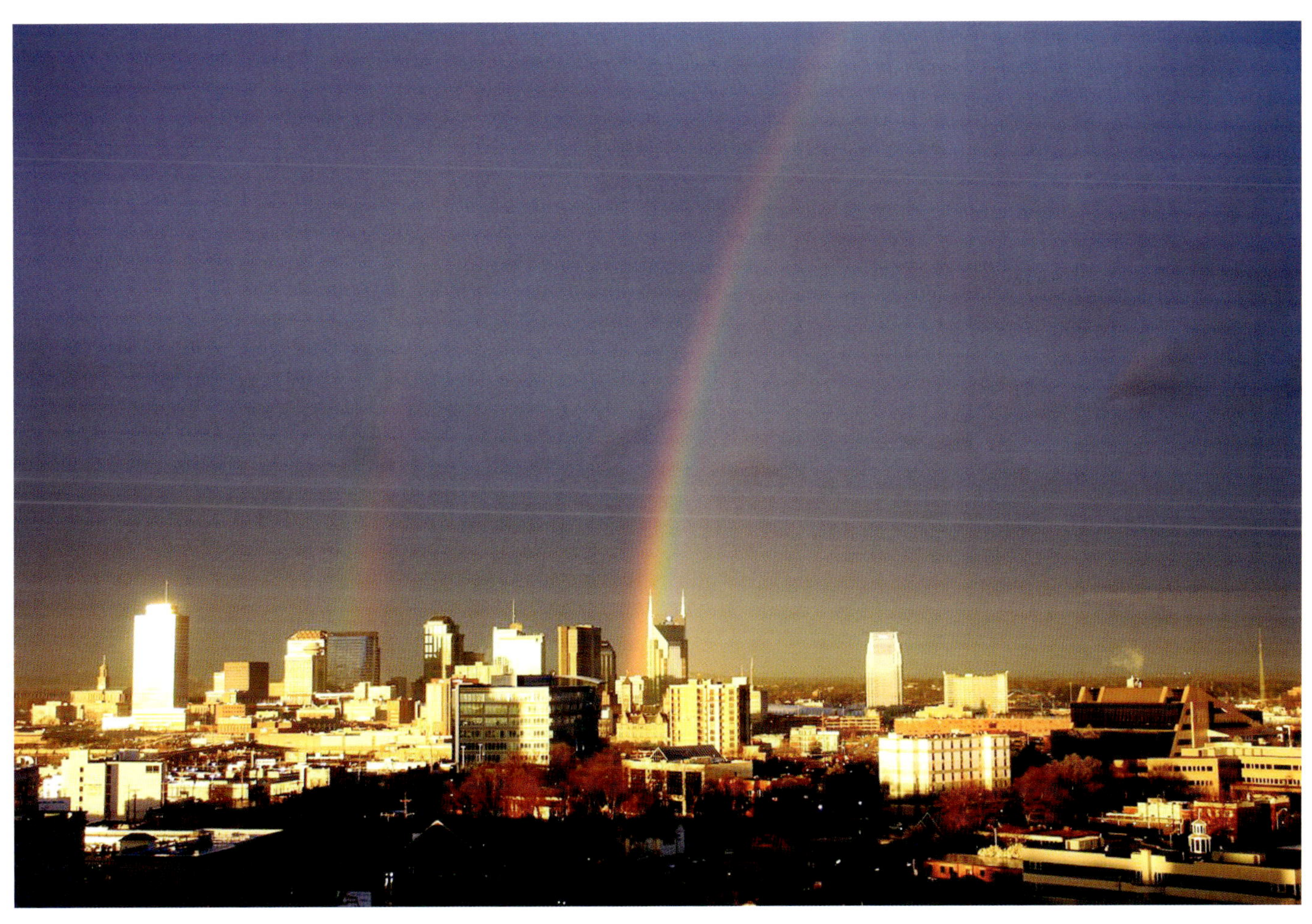

James Terry
Nashville, Tennessee, 2014

CHECKLIST OF THE EXHIBITION

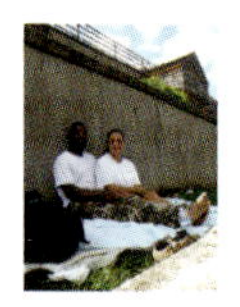

Holly Abernathy
Listening to the Game Across the River, 2018

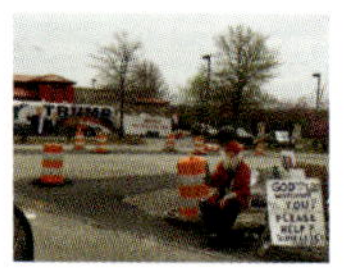

Martha Armstrong
Make Bellevue Great Again, 2017

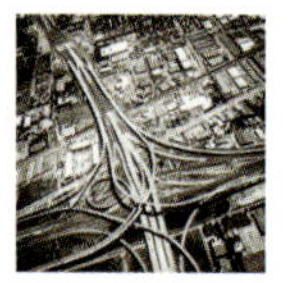

Kim Balevre
Spaghetti Junction, 2016

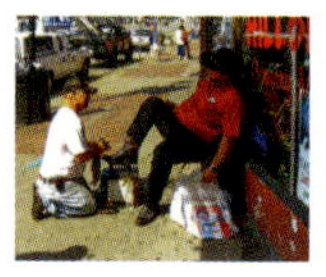

David Bennett
Lower Broadway, 2018

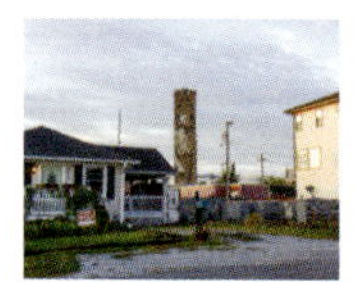

Elizabeth Berger
Mr. Estes Ponders Progress, 2018

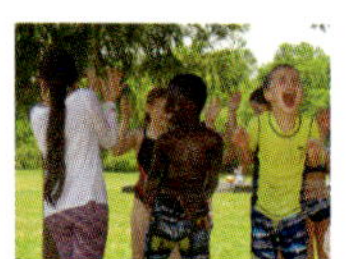

Mariah Clemons
Friends Enjoying the Spray, 2017

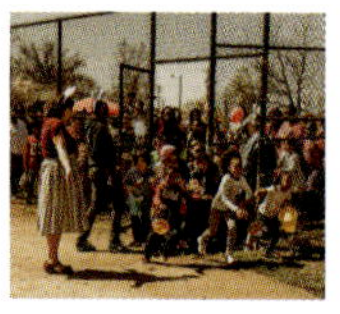

Rae'chel Curtis
East Nashville Easter Community Outreach, 2018

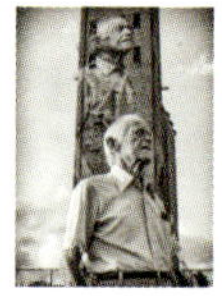

James DeMain
Mr. Estes, 2018

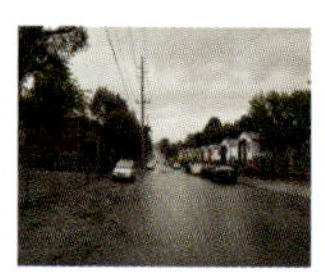

D'Anelle Desire
Connect/Disconnect, 2018

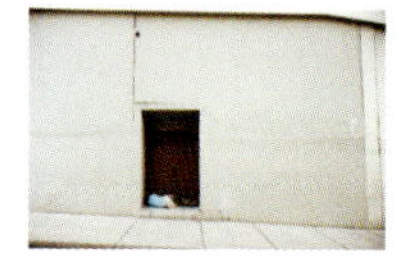

Ray Di Pietro
This Doorway Was His Home, 2018

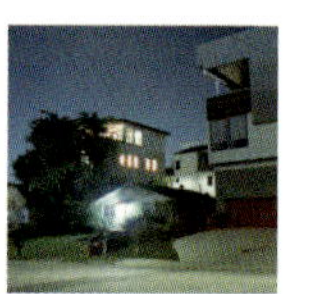

Erik Doty
New Neighbors, 2018

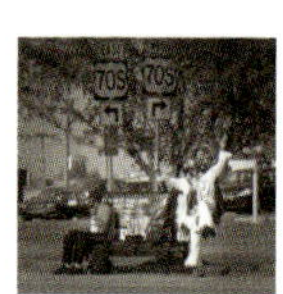

Jo Fields
Life Is . . ., 2018

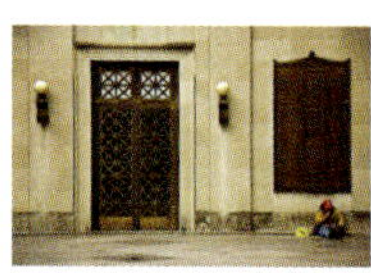

Jacqueline Flynn
Homeless in a Booming City, 2016

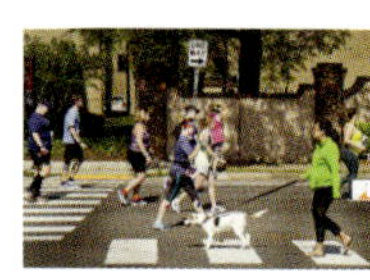

Denise Fussell
One Way, 2018

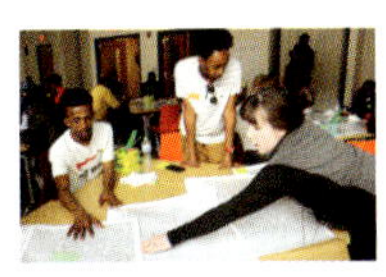

Tony Gonzalez
Visioning, 2016

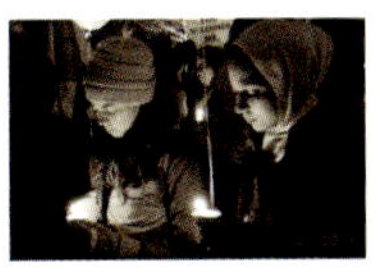

Caroline Gumpenberger
Solidarity by Candlelight, 2015

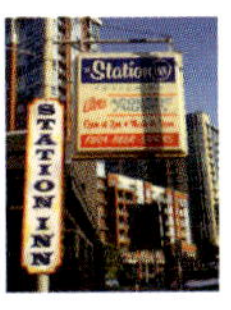

Betty Harper
Grandfathered Inn, 2017

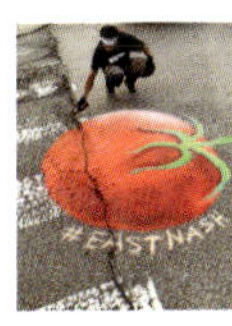

Alan Hayes
Street Mural in East Nashville, 2018

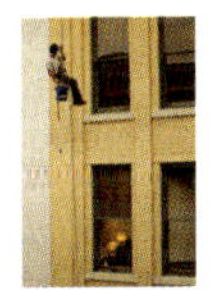

Bernadette Hugan
Tethered, 2018

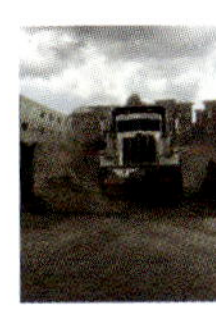

D. Elizabeth Jesse
Nashville on the Move, 2018

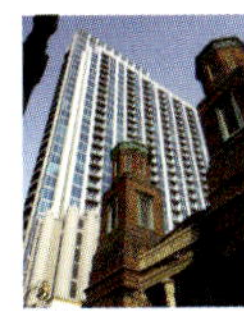

Lisa Sivess Johnson
House of God, 2014

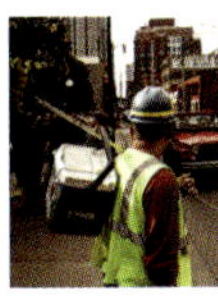

DaShawn Lewis
Common Practices, 2018

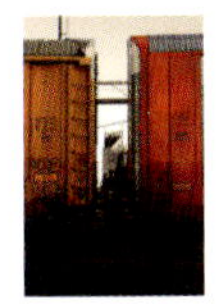

Kevin Lurey
The Bench, 2018

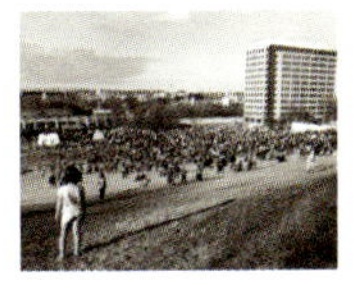

Hamilton Masters
Future, 2018

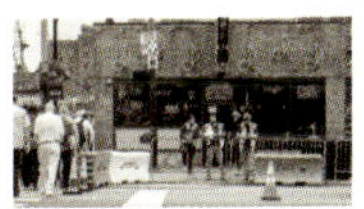

Kalonji McClellan
Downtown Changing, 2018

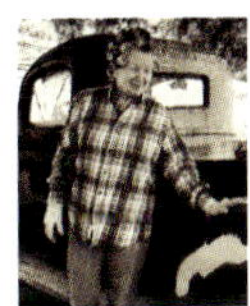

Erin McDermott
Working Woman, 2018

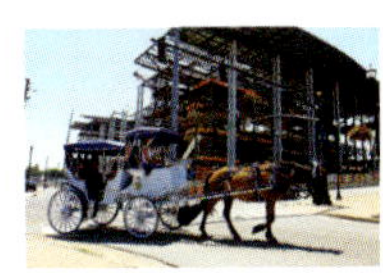

Don McEwen
Music City Center, 2011

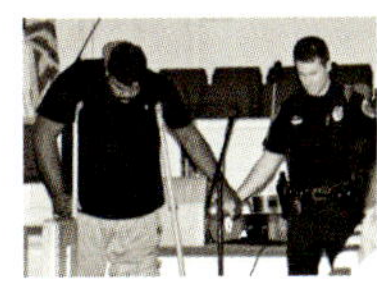

Donna Moffitt
Rise Above, 2016

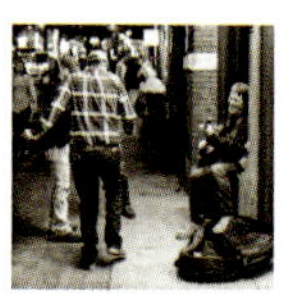

David Morel
When the Music Moves You, 2016

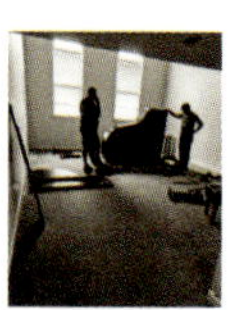

Justin Near
Piano Moving, 2018

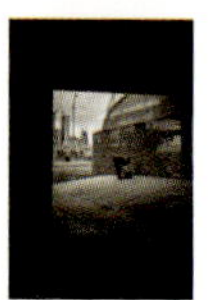

Joshua Ness
The Outskirts, 2018

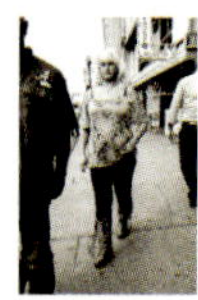

Huy Nguyen
Uncertainty, 2018

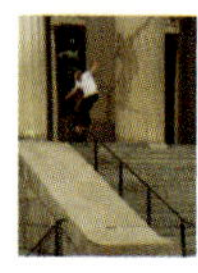

Joe Nuñez
Jamie Foy Front Feeble, 2018

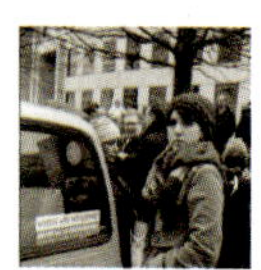

Emily Passino
Where Are We Going, 2017

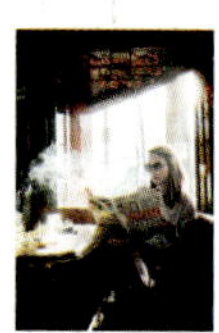

Julia Lynn Perkins
Extra, Extra, 2018

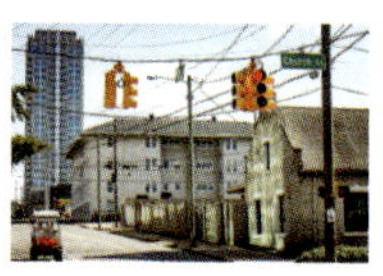

Mary Phelps
17th & Church, 2018

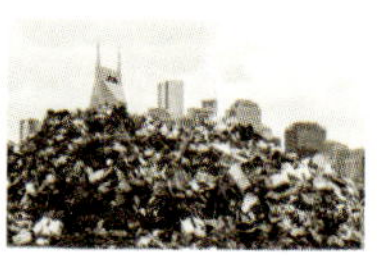

David Piñeros
Under the Music City, 2018

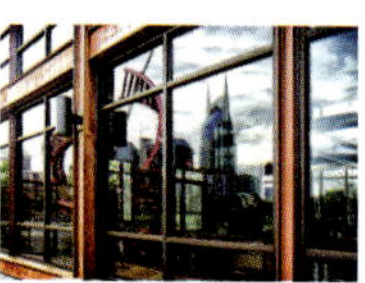

John Roeder
Nashville Skyline East View, 2013

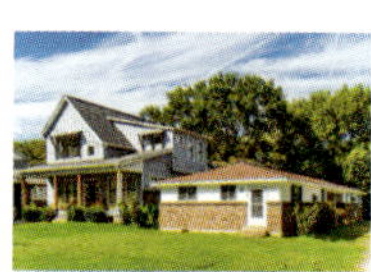

Carey Rogers
Photo 2, 2018

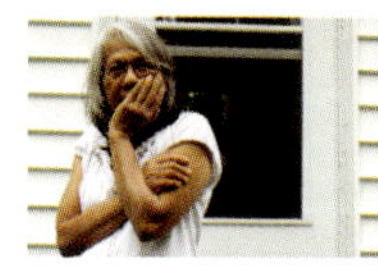

Delia Seigenthaler
Udom, Thompson Lane, 2018

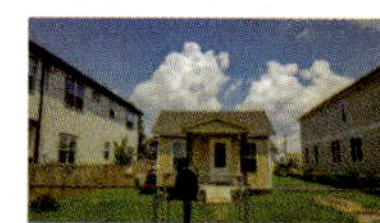

Brian Siskind
The Nations Life, 2016

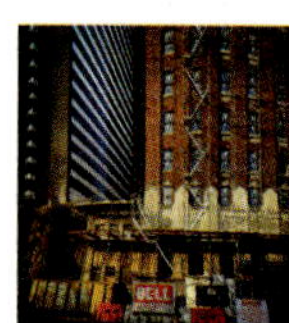

Gene Smith
Modernize or Else, 2017

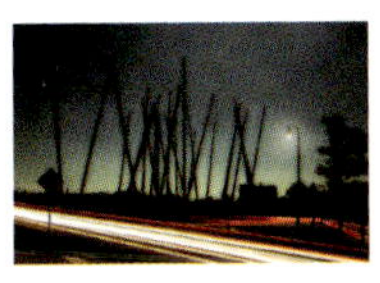

Ben Spalding
Nashville Stix Roundabout, 2018

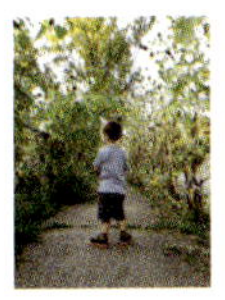

Laura Sturgill
Show Me the Way, 2018

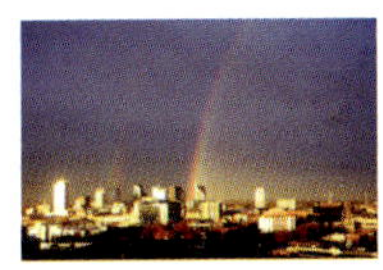

James Terry
Nashville, Tennessee, 2014

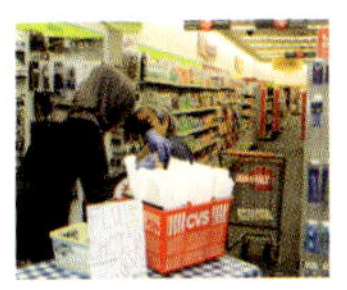

Yukiko Ueda
Free Flu Shot, 2017

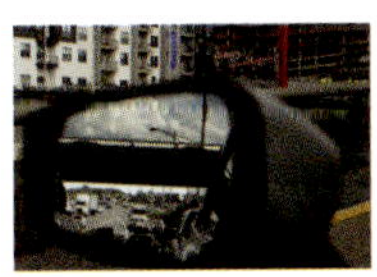

Ramona Wiggins
Growing Pains in the "It City," 2018

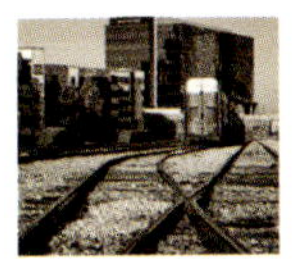

Richard Wise
Train Tracks, 2017

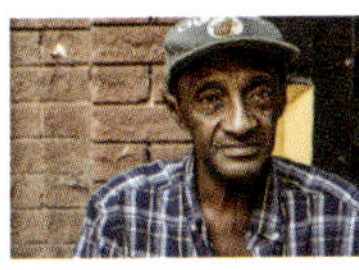

Nick Zimmer
Disconnect, 2016